LILY VANILLI'S
SWEET TOOTH

Since she started out selling her cakes at a market in East London, Lily Jones (aka Vanilli) has gone on to become one of Britain's best-loved artisan bakers. With a star-studded client list, Lily's bakes are famous for their unique flavour combinations, spectacular design and exquisite taste. In 2011 she opened her first bakery on Columbia Road in East London. She runs a cake and cocktail private members club and is one of the founders of The YBF Awards. She is also the author of *A Zombie Ate My Cupcake*.

LILY VANILLI'S

SWEET TOOTH

RECIPES AND TIPS FROM A MODERN ARTISAN BAKERY

LILY JONES

PHOTOGRAPHY BY ROMAS FOORD

CANONGATE

Published in Great Britain in 2012 by Canongate Books Ltd,
14 High Street, Edinburgh EH1 1TE

www.canongate.tv

2

British Library Cataloguing-in-Publication Data
A catalogue record for this book is available on
request from the British Library

ISBN 978 0 85786 441 3

Editor: Jenny Lord
Art direction: Rafaela Romaya
Design: Two Associates
Photography: Romas Foord
Styling: Lily Jones
Illustration (p36-37): Katherine Pont

Printed in China on acid-free paper by C&C Offset Printing Co., Ltd

FOR DAVID

CONTENTS

INTRODUCTION

For a long time baking was a hobby, until one summer, unable to find a job and fast running out of savings, I started selling a few cakes I'd made in my home kitchen at a small market in East London. The pitch cost me £10, and I'd come home with £30 or £40 each week. It was a way to make a bit of extra cash; I had no expansion plans, no loan, no projected sales and no PR. I never did make more than £40 in a week at Swanfield market, but my cakes were noticed by a food writer for *The Times*. She wrote an article that was published in February 2009, and Lily Vanilli was born.

Since then I have supplied Harrods with cakes, tarts and brownies, made canapés for Elton John's 'White Tie and Tiara Ball', made a cake sculpture that was displayed at the V&A (spiced dark chocolate with grapefruit mousse and Buck's Fizz curd) and opened the Lily Vanilli Bakery on Columbia Road in East London, which now employs a staff of seven. From those few little cakes I used to sell at Swanfield market, our bakery is now producing hundreds of pies, tarts, sausage rolls, ice creams and cakes every week. During the week we use the space to make bespoke cake sculptures, sweet canapés and bake for private orders, and every Sunday we open our doors to hundreds of locals and tourists visiting the famous East End flower market.

🍒

I have no formal training or background in food; my real passion for baking grew from a simple desire to make myself perfect desserts. I've always thought that if I'm going to eat something as indulgent as cake it ought to be exactly how I like it, with just the right balance of sweet, light, nutty or fruity. For this reason my recipes are always evolving, or changing with the seasons – like my carrot cake, which changes between

summer and winter (as the days get shorter, I'll make it richer and spicier, with healthy amounts of brandy – see pages 58–59 for the recipe).

Everything I know about baking I have learned through trial and error, through reading and practice. Because I'm self-taught, I have always been free to experiment, applying my own touches to recipes and preparing cakes, biscuits and pies with ingredients I have to hand, or that catch my eye in the shop. My vanilla and pomegranate cake, which won Gold at the Great Taste Awards, would never have come about if I hadn't had a beautiful ruby red pomegranate sitting cut open on the kitchen counter one morning.

Baking can be a great way to express yourself, and if you treat it this way, your baking will always be unique. The food you make should be adapted to suit your taste or the tastes of the people you are baking for. When baking for friends and customers I always apply this philosophy – I ask them exactly how they'd like

their dream cake to look and taste, and make it as close to perfect for them as I can.

People often talk about baking being a science, but don't let this put you off. The methods we use today weren't developed by men in lab coats, they were born of trial and error, from the enthusiasm, passion and experimentation of generations of bakers like you and me. There are countless examples of well-loved desserts that were born out of mix-ups in the kitchen which prove this, such as the Bakewell tart and the brownie.

However, baking in the twenty-first century we now have the benefit of a scientific understanding of what we're doing. When you make a cake, a meringue or a custard, you are in control of specific physical and chemical processes, which if handled right will produce the desired effect. So while it's important to feel free to experiment, it's helpful to embrace the science too: an understanding of the basic rules will give you a head start in producing a cake with the right texture, a pastry with the right flakiness, or a custard with the perfect consistency. And it's not just practical – discovering the science behind what I'm baking has always held a huge fascination for me.

I'm often asked for my top baking tips, and my answer usually disappoints. I say there are some fundamental techniques that should be learned, and a few steps that shouldn't be skipped – a little bit of hard work at the beginning that really pays off. I could tell you to scrape the bottom of the mixing bowl and handle pastry lightly, but only by understanding why you need to do these things can you really become a better baker. Once you know when you need to be strict with a recipe, you can start to enjoy its freedom. Once you've mastered some of the core techniques, you have armed yourself with the knowledge required to prepare hundreds of diverse dishes, each stamped with your own individual personality and taste.

With that in mind I have divided this book into sections, each explaining a simple method and demonstrating some of the varied things you can make with this core knowledge. I will demonstrate with my own recipes how far you can take basic techniques in your home kitchen, where I learned them myself

not so long ago. From a simple custard you can go on to make dishes as diverse as absinthe and dark mint chocolate chip ice cream | see page 247 |, a decadent sherry trifle | page 85 | or a spiced apple custard tart | page 127 | – and with little more effort than it would take to make a cupcake. At the core of baking there's an exact science, but each dish you create is something personal, an act of generosity, a celebration or an indulgence. My top baking tip is: learn the basics, and then make the recipe your own. Hopefully the techniques and recipes in this book are a good place to start.

A NOTE ON USING THIS BOOK

At the back of the book, on pages 254–261, you will find a number of core recipes – coulis, buttercream, frangipane, custard and ganache – that are used and adapted throughout the book to create a whole range of very different things. You can use these basics as building blocks for your own desserts too. The book is divided into sections, each exploring a core method and explaining some of the techniques and science behind it in more detail. It's fine to skip these bits and dive straight into the recipes; you will still get great results. But hopefully reading them will help you to progress your baking skills, understand why things go wrong if they do, and arm yourself with the confidence to start adapting recipes to suit your tastes.

BEFORE YOU START

INGREDIENTS

Understanding the ingredients you're working with will help you become
a better baker. This section looks at some core ingredients.

SUGAR

SUGAR will work its way in some form into most of the sweet things you make. It does more than add sweetness: depending on the recipe, sugar can add moisture, tenderness, stability, act as a preservative, enhance other flavours and caramelise. Understanding more about how different sugars can affect what you're baking will help you to choose them confidently and adapt a recipe to suit you. Here is a list of some of the sugars and their uses.

GRANULATED: An all-purpose sugar, highly sweet and with a very simple flavour. It has larger crystals than caster sugar, and while it can be used in most recipes as a substitute if you're really stuck, it's not ideal unless specified.

CASTER: A very finely ground sugar that dissolves faster than white granulated sugar, and creams more readily. It is especially useful for making meringues and for creaming butter and sugar to form the basis of sponge cakes. If you don't have any caster sugar around, you can make your own by grinding granulated sugar for a couple of minutes in a food processor (just give it a couple of seconds to settle before opening the lid to avoid clouds of sugar dust).

GOLDEN CASTER SUGAR: White sugar with added molasses: it can be substituted for caster sugar in any recipe and will give it a fuller, slightly caramel flavour.

LIGHT/DARK BROWN SUGAR: Another caster sugar with added molasses, this adds colour as well as a deeper caramel flavour. It's very moist and will increase the tenderness of a cake. Store sealed in a cool dry place to prevent it from drying out.

MUSCOVADO: A type of unrefined natural sugar, available in light or dark brown, that has a strong flavour of natural molasses. Its colour and flavour come from sugarcane juice left in during the production process; as a result it is sticky, but can be used like any other brown sugar.

The sugars above can be substituted for each other in most cases, and although this will affect the bake, it shouldn't spoil what you are making. Experiment with substituting sugars to see how flavour and texture are affected – try making a meringue with golden caster sugar and you will see that it has a much deeper flavour, while a sponge made with dark brown sugar will have a denser and softer texture.

ICING SUGAR/CONFECTIONERS' SUGAR: Granulated sugar that has been ground to a fine powder, often with cornflour added to prevent clumping and crystallisation. It dissolves very rapidly and is good for making icing and buttercream, and for dusting finished cakes.

UNREFINED SOFT BROWN SUGAR: These sugars have a distinctive caramel taste. Light and dark soft brown sugars have different flavour and moistness properties, so you can only replace one with the other in small quantities.

MOLASSES: A by-product of sugar manufacturing, this dark syrup is less sweet than sugar and has its own strong flavour and more acidity.

HONEY: In some cake recipes honey can be substituted for granulated or caster sugar and will produce a moist and dense cake, but you will need to reduce the amount, as it is much sweeter and browns faster. Try using approximately half the amount of honey to sugar, reducing the liquid in the recipe accordingly, and lower the oven temperature slightly too.

LIQUID GLUCOSE: A syrupy sweetener. It inhibits crystallisation of sugars, so is useful for making sorbets, jams and hard candies.

GOLDEN SYRUP: An inverted sugar syrup that is much sweeter than sugar, this also has a slightly caramel flavour. It can also be used to a lesser extent to help inhibit crystallisation of sugar. Perfect for making gingerbread and flapjacks.

FLOUR

FLOUR provides the foundation for most baked goods. It gives structure, texture and to some extent flavour.

CHOOSING FLOUR

One of the key things to know about flour is that it contains proteins which when combined with liquid form gluten | see right |. The type of flour you choose and the method for each recipe will be largely affected by how much gluten you want to develop. Most of the recipes in this book use plain flour and a method that encourages minimal gluten development, for light, airy cakes and flaky pastries. I try to use organic flours where possible, as they are of better quality and give better results. Here's a list of some types of flour and their uses.

PLAIN WHITE FLOUR: This is the flour you will use for most of the recipes in this book; it's a soft flour with a low protein content suited to making pastries and cakes. Plain flour is formed when the bran is removed from wholemeal flour | see below |.

SELF-RAISING WHITE FLOUR: A pre-made combination of plain white flour and a chemical leavener (a raising agent such as baking powder). You can make a decent substitute for self-raising flour by adding 1 teaspoon of baking powder for every 120g of plain flour. Make sure you combine them evenly before adding them to a batter.

WHOLEMEAL FLOUR: This includes the nutritious wheat germ and bran from the wholegrain wheat; the amount of wholegrain that is retained varies (all the way up to 100%), and the percentage will be stated on the packet. Wholemeal flour can be plain or self-raising.

SPELT: We use spelt flour a lot at the bakery. An ancient precursor of modern wheat, it has a beautiful rich, slightly nutty flavour, and while it does contain gluten, it is often found to be gentle on people with a gluten intolerance.

BREAD FLOUR: Often labelled as 'strong' flour, bread flour is ground from 'hard' wheat with a high content of gluten, which contributes elasticity to a dough.

WHY SIFT FLOUR?

The importance of sifting flour divides opinion among bakers – many swear they never do it and their bakes don't suffer as a result. I personally sift flour at least once, partly because I like doing it but also because it aerates the flour and loosens up any clumps to ensure it absorbs liquid evenly. It is another step you can take towards perfecting a light, evenly risen cake.

STORING FLOUR

Flour is best used relatively 'fresh', so avoid stockpiling or baking with flour that has been knocking about in the back of your cupboard for ever. Buy flour in smaller batches and try to use it within three months. Store airtight in a cool place.

GLUTEN

GLUTEN is formed when two proteins found in flour come into contact with liquid and combine, like a two-part glue. Exposure to heat and friction will develop gluten to build a web-like network of elastic and expansible strands within your dough or batter. This network traps air pockets and forms the structure of your bake.

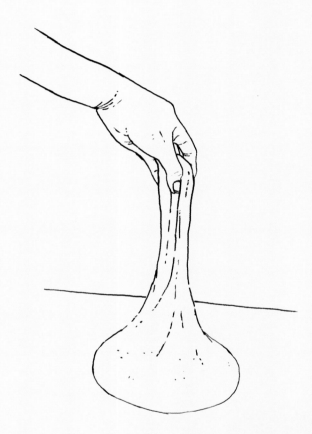

The more gluten is 'developed' (by mixing or kneading), the stronger and longer the strands get, giving your bake a chewy and tough texture – desirable in bread but not in pastry or cakes. The illustration above shows a dough with a well developed gluten structure. In many recipes, specific methods are put in place just to inhibit the development of gluten beyond the bare minimum necessary for building a supportive structure – for example, minimal handling and the use of cold equipment and ingredients, or coating flour in butter to limit the amount of liquid that reaches it.

BUTTER

DEPENDING on how it's used and what you're baking, butter plays many different roles, but in general it tenderises, adds flavour and helps keep your bakes fresh. Below are a few things to know about butter, and on page 153 you can learn how to make your own.

ROOM TEMPERATURE BUTTER AND HOW TO ACHIEVE IT

When a recipe calls for room temperature butter, it should be soft enough for you to easily depress the surface with your finger, but not melted. The best way to achieve this is to leave the butter out of the fridge for about an hour before you bake. If you're caught out, you can cut cold butter into 2.5cm cubes and heat it either in a microwave (at 10-second intervals, keeping an eye on it until it reaches the right consistency), or in a heavy-bottomed pan over a low heat until no more than a third is melted and the rest is soft (you can turn the heat off and leave it once the pan is hot). You can also leave the butter, in a dish, in a warm place like an airing cupboard or on top of the oven, but don't forget about it.

WHY UNSALTED BUTTER?

There are a number of reasons why unsalted butter is specified in most baking recipes, and it's not just to do with flavour. The amount of salt and the water content vary greatly between salted butters, making it harder to be precise. Salt and liquid also play a role in the toughening of gluten, which is something you want to keep in control of while you bake | see page 19 for more on this |, and unsalted butter is likely to be fresher and purer, as it is not destined for the long shelf life that salted butter has.

EGGS

EGGS are the backbone of most baked goods – they contribute to their structure, provide steam for leavening and add moisture for gluten development. Egg yolks add tenderising fat and help to emulsify a batter, which gives things a smooth and creamy texture. Egg whites act as strengtheners, and help to trap air in a batter, which makes it rise and gives it an even crumb.

CHOOSING EGGS

Always try to use free-range eggs – you shouldn't have any trouble finding them, as caged eggs are now illegal in the UK. Eggs come in different sizes – I use UK medium eggs (approximately 50g – whites 35g, yolks 15g) for the recipes in this book unless otherwise specified. Most baking recipes will call for room temperature eggs, so make sure you leave them out of the fridge before using them – alternatively you can bring their temperature up by placing them in a bowl of tepid water.

HOW TO SEPARATE EGGS

Techniques differ, but I tap the top of the shell sharply with a heavy knife for a clean break, then tip the yolk between the two halves of the shell, draining out the white as I go. Eggs are easier to separate if they are cold, so if you're having difficulties, separate them straight from the fridge and allow them to come to room temperature before you use them.

THINGS TO DO WITH LEFTOVER EGG WHITES OR YOLKS

You can keep leftover whites or yolks for up to three days in the fridge if sealed. You can also freeze them airtight for up to three months. Remember to label the container with either the weight or the number of yolks or whites.

SAVE LEFTOVER WHITES FOR: Meringues, macaroons.
SAVE LEFTOVER YOLKS FOR: Custard, ice cream, egg wash, pastry.

AIR

ALTHOUGH not usually listed as an ingredient, air is essential to many recipes and a lot of the methods and ingredients used in baking are there specifically to trap and retain it. The air in your batter will affect the texture, size and appearance of the finished bake. Air bubbles trapped in egg whites will lift a cake, as will the air trapped in the creaming stage of baking. Leavenings such as bicarbonate of soda, baking powder and yeast release carbon dioxide in the oven, which assists the rise of a cake and can add a lightness to denser bakes like biscuits. Whichever way they're incorporated, it's gas expanding in those air bubbles when heated that causes the cake batter to rise.

EQUIPMENT

We all grow up with a few mottos that have been drilled into us from childhood, and mine was 'A bad workman blames his tools.' When it comes to baking, you don't need a lot of fancy equipment. The right tools will help you do a good job, but if you're resourceful you can get by with a few essentials. Which brings me to the first tool on the list – your hands. Don't be afraid to get your hands dirty when you bake, as they're often the best tool for the job – scooping and spreading batters, making and kneading doughs, smoothing, patting, testing for doneness, moulding and portioning.

CORE TOOLS

HEAVY-BOTTOMED PAN: For heating syrups, sauces and sugars, and for making a double boiler | otherwise known as a bain-marie – see page 196 |.

SIEVE: Fine metal for sifting flour and coarser metal for passing custards, sauces and coulis – anything that requires a smooth, consistent texture.

MIXING BOWLS: Metal is best, followed by glass and then plastic. Having extra bowls is a real luxury, as it saves washing and drying mid-bake, but you will get by with two good-sized bowls. At least one should hold 5 litres and both should hold a minimum of 3 litres.

METAL BALLOON WHISK: Useful for whisking liquids and also for evenly mixing together any dry ingredients you are adding in one go.

STAND MIXER: With a whisk and paddle attachment, a stand mixer will make your life much easier. I got by for a long time with just a hand-held electric whisk (which kept breaking), but my baking got a lot easier (and tidier) when I could finally afford a stand mixer. My Kenwood Chef served me incredibly well – I stayed up with that mixer many a long night making literally thousands of cakes, one small batch at a time.

GOOD SCALES: A good set of scales that measures in grams, ounces and millilitres can be bought for around £15 and will suit your home baking needs perfectly. Look for one that measures up to 2.2kg in 1g increments and has a flat surface rather than a built-in bowl.

SILICONE SPATULA: An indispensable item for any baker. Scraping down the bowl with a spatula as you make up your batters should be a habit you get into, especially if you are using a stand mixer. A spatula is also useful for folding and for reaching into the very edge of a pot that needs stirring. Silicone is heat-resistant up to 260°C, so can be used to stir very hot liquids.

MEASURING SPOONS: Useful for accurate measuring of 1 tablespoon, 1 teaspoon, ½ teaspoon and ¼ teaspoon. If you're caught short, it's useful to know that 1 tablespoon is equal to 3 teaspoons.

BAKING PAPER: Use silicone or parchment paper for baking, not greaseproof – it works much better.

BAKING TRAYS: Useful not only for baking biscuits and meringues, but for chocolate and sugar work too.

TART TINS AND CAKE TINS: A range of sizes might be useful, as using the wrong size of tin will affect your bake | see page 24 |. The material a tin is made from can also affect it – I recommend aluminium tins, which distribute heat well.

OVEN: This is one piece of equipment you will probably have to make do with. Every oven I've ever used has had its own personality and nuances. In the bakery we have two ovens – 'Wild Bill', who is great for baking bread and roasting but will blow everything around and burn it if you're not very careful, and 'The Perv', so named because this one has a little light you can push to peek inside.

OVEN THERMOMETER: Ovens vary greatly, and I've never moved into a kitchen – home or professional – where the ovens are set to the right temperature. Before you bake anything, you should check your oven temperature with a thermometer. Do some experimenting and work out how the temperature of the oven relates to the temperature on the dial. Test the temperature of different shelves and parts of the oven to ascertain the heat distribution – often the top shelf will be hotter, so cakes on that shelf will bake quicker. I worked with a standard home oven for a long time and got to know exactly when to rotate a tray or switch cakes between shelves. You will get to know your oven better than anyone, and will likely need to adapt baking times accordingly.

NOTE: The oven temperatures in this book are for a fan-assisted (convection) home oven. If you are using a conventional home oven you should increase oven temperature by 20°C. Remember – every oven is different, so test the temperature with a thermometer or prepare for a few practice runs to get it right. Conventional ovens are also more likely to have 'hot spots' | see above |.

A NOTE ON TIN SIZES

One of the last things people think to check when trying out a new recipe is whether they have the right tin, and it's tempting just to tip the batter in and hope for the best. But this can really affect the outcome of your cake – if the tin is too full the cake might not be able to support its own weight as it rises and might collapse, or it could spill over the edges. If it's too shallow it could burn. Make sure you check the specified tin size and use the correct one – it might be worth investing in a few new tins if you plan to do a lot of baking, or you can scale your recipe up or down to fit the tin you have.

OTHER USEFUL TOOLS

PLASTIC PASTRY SCRAPER: My favourite tool in the kitchen; frustrating, as these are not generally available to the home baker, but get hold of one and it will become your best friend. I use it for scraping down bowls, separating dough, scooping batter into tins and scraping down surfaces when I've finished and made a mess. You won't find them in homeware shops, but you can get them very inexpensively online | see page 263 for stockists |.

MEASURING JUG: A good set of scales will measure in millilitres, but it's handy to have a jug of some kind around for adding liquids gradually.

GRATER: For grating vegetables. You can also use a food processor, but it will often grate much finer than you need.

ZESTER: For chocolate and fruits.

FOOD PROCESSOR: Handy (but not essential) for making up doughs, chopping and grinding nuts and whizzing up liquids with solids.

PALETTE KNIFE: For spreading chocolate and icing cakes.

WOODEN SPOON: To stir anything you're heating on the stove, though a silicone spatula will work just as well.

WIRE COOLING RACK: The best way to cool cakes – it ensures air can get to the cake from all angles, so that it cools evenly and doesn't go soggy at the bottom.

PIPING BAG: A piping bag will make your desserts (and you) look professional. A re-usable bag and one or two tips are all you need to decorate the cakes in this book. | See page 26 for how to use a piping bag |.

COPPER BOWL: Best for whipping egg whites.

GOOD OVEN GLOVES: These should be heat-resistant and not so cumbersome that you lose your dexterity in getting cakes or tart bases out of the oven without damaging them.

SUGAR THERMOMETER: When you're working with boiled sugar, you will need to invest in one of these to help you control the temperature | see page 213 for more |.

SILICONE ROLLING PIN: For pastry, doughs and fondant.

ADDITIONAL HANDY TOOLS

- Cocktail sticks – for testing when your cakes are done
- Knives, forks, spoons and kitchen scissors
- Pestle and mortar
- Biscuit cutters
- Oven timer
- Baking beans for blind baking
- Kitchen roll, clingfilm and tin foil

A NOTE ON CLINGING PROPERLY

Storing things airtight is key to achieving their maximum shelf life – if you're using clingfilm to wrap leftover icing, batters, coulis, custard or anything else liquid, press the clingfilm to the surface of the liquid, not just across the top of the bowl, to seal it airtight. If you're wrapping anything dry, make sure you wrap it, not the bowl.

USING A PIPING BAG

PIPING bags are handy for icing, filling tarts and buns, and piping perfect cookies, chocolate and meringues. It takes a bit of getting the hang of, but with a little practice you'll get it in no time. Here's how you do it.

Slip the nozzle into place, following the instructions that come with your bag. Hold the bag about 10cm above the nozzle and pull the rest of the bag down over your hand like a cuff. Use a spatula, wooden spoon or large metal serving spoon to scoop some of whatever it is you are piping into the nose of the bag. Bring the cuff back up and push the batter down towards the nozzle, working out any air pockets that might have got trapped. Twist the bag above the batter and hold it there with your right hand (or your left if you are left-handed). Squeeze from here and use the other hand to guide your piping.

TOP TIP: SPLITTING THE BAG

This is one of the best baking tips I was ever given. If the bag is too full, heavy or stiff for you to be able to get a good flow with your piping, split the bag by twisting it halfway through the batter (taking care the rest doesn't spill out of the top). You can then hold the top of the bag with your left hand (if right-handed) and pipe from the split with your right as normal. This will mean you don't have to keep refilling the bag and you can handle piping even when you have weak wrists like mine.

WHICH NOZZLE DO I USE?

- 1M (1.5cm open star) — good for piping swirls, roses, meringues, cookies and icing cupcakes.
- Wilton 10 (medium round tip) — useful for piping edges and making meringue mushrooms | page 191 | and bones | page 185 |.
- Wilton 5 (smallish round tip) — useful for piping thin lines and dabs of frosting or chocolate.
- 104 (ruffle tip) — makes a nice ruffle effect for decorating cakes.

AND FINALLY...

- Be prepared to do the dishes! **WASHING UP** will make up about a quarter of your baking time, so it's worth a bit of planning to make sure you have the right tools clean when you need them. Be extra prepared with a sink of warm, soapy water.

- If you're organised you're less likely to make mistakes – prepare your utensils in advance, **READ THROUGH A RECIPE FROM START TO FINISH** before you begin, even if it's something you've made before, and try to clean up as you go. The results will show in your baking.

- **MAKE SPACE TO WORK**. If you have a small kitchen, look for ways to make extra surface space – clear your dining table or pull in another table from somewhere.

- **KEEP A STOCK OF THE BASICS**, especially free-range eggs, unsalted butter, caster sugar, plain flour and baking powder. You're more likely to experiment and learn if you can whip something up when the mood takes you.

- **CHECK YOUR INGREDIENTS ARE AT THE RIGHT TEMPERATURE**. Different recipes call for ingredients at different temperatures, and getting them wrong or right will greatly affect the outcome of your bake. Butter that's too cold can be chopped into small cubes and gently heated in a pan or microwave. Cold eggs can be brought to room temperature by placing them in a dish of tepid (not boiling) water.

- **PREHEAT YOUR OVEN** to the right temperature for at least 20 minutes before you need to use it. Check all the shelves are in the right place and try to keep the door closed – open it only when putting your bakes in and resist opening the door during bake time, as the cold air of the room will lower the oven temperature.

- **PREPARE ANY TINS** you will be using before you start.

- **LEARN TO TRUST YOUR INSTINCTS**. Get to know your oven and all its quirks inside out, so you learn when to rotate your baking trays or switch cake tins between shelves to ensure an even bake. When I started out making cakes for other people I was baking from home and I would bake hundreds of batches a day in my tiny oven; I never used a timer, but I always knew when a cake was ready by the smell that filled the room.

CAKE

ULTIMATE PILLOW-SOFT VANILLA SPONGE CAKE 38 • LAVENDER AND TOASTED ALMOND TEA CAKES 41 • PASSIONFRUIT AND TOASTED ALMOND TEA CAKES 41 • VANILLA POMEGRANATE LAYER CAKE 41 • VANILLA COCOA TEA CAKES 44 • COCONUT TEA CAKES 44 • MIXED BERRY VICTORIA SPONGE 45 • GLITTER CAKE AND COOKIE CANAPÉS 45 • BITTER CHOCOLATE ORANGE CAKE 46• CHERRY AND SEED MADEIRA CAKE 48 • ZEBRA CAKE 52 • BEETROOT CAKE 55 • FLOURLESS OREO CAKE 56 • SUMMER/WINTER CARROT CAKE 58 • APPLE AND ROSEMARY OLIVE OIL CAKE 61• CHOCOLATE AVOCADO CAKE 62 • MARGARITA DRIZZLE CAKE 65 • PORTER CAKE 66 • SIMPLE DECADENT CHOCOLATE CAKE 69 • PEAR, PARSNIP AND GINGER CAKE 70 • RED VELVET 72 • MINI LAYER CAKE CANAPÉS 73 • RED VELVET LAYER CAKE 74 • BLEEDING HEARTS 77 • FLOURLESS CHOCOLATE AFTER DINNER CAKE 78 • HAZELNUT AND PINEAPPLE UPSIDE-DOWN CAKE 81 • GLUTEN-FREE CARROT AND COURGETTE CAKE 82 • VERY BOOZY SHERRY TRIFLE 85 • ROSES CAKE 87 • CAKE WITH EDIBLE FLOWERS 88 • CHOCOLATE DECORATED CAKE 89 • GLITTER LETTER CAKE 90 • LUSTRE FRUIT CAKE 91 • SHATTERED GLASS CAKE 92 • STAINED GLASS CAKE 93

SPONGE CAKE

SPONGE recipes began to appear in the 1600s, when ovens were improving and new types of leavening were being experimented with. Before that, the closest thing to cake was a sweetened, enriched, spiced bread.

A sponge recipe generally contains flour, sugar, fat, eggs, a raising agent and some liquid, and is made using the 'creaming method'. Understanding this method and the basic ingredients for a sponge should give you a good intro to the 'ins and outs' of baking cakes. You may want to skip this part and go straight to the recipe: you will still get a good result. I have always been fascinated by the science behind every step and measure and have found that understanding it (or trying to) makes the whole process more involving and leads to much better results. There are more rules for a baker than for a chef, and whether you follow them or not, it can be really useful to try to understand them.

BALANCING THE CORE INGREDIENTS

Flour and eggs are the backbone of a cake; they give it structure, but can also dry it out. Sugar and fats make it soft and moist but can destroy its structure. A good sponge cake needs a careful balance of the core ingredients.

A NOTE ON FAT IN CAKES

Oil greases the proteins found in flour much better than butter does and makes for a more moist, tender cake; however, there is a difference in flavour. Experiment with replacing some of the butter in cake recipes with oil.

STEP 1: CREAMING THE FAT AND SUGAR

'Creaming' involves beating together the fat (butter) and the sugar and ensures that your cake will have a fine, even texture. Beating drives the sugar crystals into the butter, and their rough edges catch lots of tiny regular pockets of air that are trapped in a coating layer of fat. These pockets form the basis of the cake. (Caster sugar is best here, as its smaller crystals result in a higher number of smaller air pockets.) Eventually each of those little pockets of air will fill up with expanding gas and steam in the oven, making it rise with a texture that's soft and light. How long this stage takes will vary according to your mixer – I recommend approximately 5 minutes, but you'll know it's ready when it looks lighter and increased in volume; this is what a recipe refers to as 'light and fluffy'.

TIP: Starting the mixer on low and then gradually increasing the speed allows the air bubbles to form and strengthen. Starting at too high a speed could break the fragile air bubbles, which will cause the finished cake to be heavy and dense.

STEP 2: BEATING IN THE EGGS

The next step is to beat in the eggs, which will seal the buttery air pockets and help prevent them from collapsing when the butter melts in the oven. Egg whites also contain proteins that set to hold the structure of the cake, and the yolks add tenderness and a creamy texture. Only beat to incorporate eggs; there's no benefit to the cake in extra beating once they have been added. Over-beating at this stage can lead to a separated cake with a shiny 'crust'.

STEP 3: ADDING THE FLOUR, BAKING POWDER AND LIQUID

Flour contains the makings of the gluten which, along with egg white, will form the foundation of the cake's structure | see notes on on page 19 |. Once flour has been added, beating should be kept to a minimum, to restrict the development of too much gluten (enough will support your cake, too much will give it a heavy, fibrous texture – more like bread).

BAKING POWDER: Should be whisked evenly into the flour before it's added to the batter | see note on chemical leaveners, right | – I find sifting them together is not enough to combine them evenly.

LIQUID: The right balance of liquid will give the cake structural support by helping to form gluten, add tenderness and convert to steam once in the oven, allowing more air to be released into the batter.

I usually carry out this stage in three parts, adding half the flour, then the liquid, then the remaining flour – this keeps the batter from splitting but prevents too much gluten forming. Just remember not to over-beat.

STEP 4: BAKING

Once exposed to the heat of the oven, the volume of your cake will increase and its structure will set. This is due to multiple events that take place in the batter. First, the heat causes the gases in the air pockets to expand, which in turn stretches out the gluten structure. At the same time the acid and alkali in the baking powder will react, releasing carbon dioxide, which will expand these pockets even further. Then, as the temperature creeps up, the liquids begin to steam and expand the air pockets once again. Eventually the egg in the batter will set (coagulate) and the gluten will lose its elasticity, sealing the structure of the cake. The sugar will then caramelise and give it a lovely brown finish. The temperature of your oven is key here – if your temperature is right, the timing of the expanding air pockets and melting of the fat should coincide with egg film coagulating and seal the air pockets in the cake's structure. If the temperature is out, these events might not sync so smoothly and your cake will be spoiled.

BICARBONATE OF SODA OR BAKING POWDER?

Bicarbonate of soda and baking powder are two kinds of chemical leavener or raising agent. When bicarbonate of soda (sodium bicarbonate) is combined with moisture and an acidic ingredient (e.g. cider vinegar, yoghurt, soured cream, chocolate, buttermilk, honey) the resulting chemical reaction releases carbon dioxide bubbles that expand in the oven and help your bakes to rise. This will start to happen as soon as you mix the bicarbonate of soda and the acid together in a batter, so try to get it into the oven quickly. Baking powder is a blend of acid (cream of tartar) and alkali (sodium bicarbonate). Although the acid and the alkali are already combined, they will only start to fully react when exposed to the heat of the oven. Which of the two leaveners you should use will depend on your other ingredients: bicarbonate of soda needs an acid to balance it (and to react with) so it's best used in a recipe containing an acidic ingredient – if you ever accidentally substitute bicarbonate of soda for baking powder in a recipe with no acid ingredient to balance it, you will notice a very bitter, soapy taste. Baking powder has a more neutral flavour. Don't try to substitute one for the other without adapting the rest of the recipe. In most cases, if a recipe asks you to use both, the baking powder is likely to be acting as the main leavener, while the bicarbonate of soda will be there to neutralise an excess of acid from the other ingredients.

NOTE: Measure chemical leaveners carefully; a little goes a long way. As a general rule you should use 1 teaspoon of baking powder or ¼ teaspoon of bicarbonate of soda per 130g of plain wheat flour.

IF YOUR OVEN IS TOO HOT the edges of the cake will crust before the middle has a chance to fully bake, leaving a soggy centre full of gases that continue to expand late in the baking process and cause your crust to crack. **IF YOUR OVEN IS TOO COLD** the fat will melt, releasing its air and leavening gases before the other elements in the batter set to hold them in place, and the cake won't rise.

COOLING

You should generally leave a cake to cool in the tin for at least 10 minutes after removing it from the oven, placed on a wire rack so that air can circulate. Cakes are softer and more fragile before they are fully cooled – the cooling process allows the flour's gelatinised starch to gel and firm up the cake, and if you try to remove it too soon, it will likely stick to the tin. If you leave the cake in the tin too long, the steam it releases will be trapped and make it soggy. After 10 minutes, remove it from the tin and leave it on the wire rack to cool. It's best to wait until the cake is completely cool before peeling away any baking paper, otherwise you might take chunks of cake off with it.

STORING

Cakes generally keep well at room temperature for a few days, thanks to the moisture-retaining properties of the butter and sugar they are made with. Icing a cake will help to preserve it for longer, as less of the cake is exposed to the air. Putting cakes into the fridge tends to dry them out, but you can freeze most cakes. Just wrap the un-iced cakes tightly in a thick layer of clingfilm and defrost at room temperature.

CAKES MADE WITH WHIPPED EGGS

OCCASIONALLY a recipe will call for whipped egg whites, and in this case the cake batter is getting some or all of its leavening from air trapped in the beaten whites. This process requires beating the whites to a rich white foam, filled with air bubbles. These expand in the oven until the egg sets and seals the air in place. When it comes to whipping egg whites for a cake the rules are strict, but don't be put off – it's actually very simple and you'll probably nail it first time. As with making meringues, you need to use room temperature eggs and separate them carefully, as fat from the yolks will spoil the process | see page 20 for how to separate eggs |. In fact any fat or grease is your enemy here, so make sure everything is really clean.

WHIPPING EGG WHITES

Ideally use a stand mixer with the whisk attachment or hand-held electric whisk to beat egg whites, and a mixing bowl large enough to hold up to eight times the volume of the whites you start with. Add a pinch of salt and start beating on a medium speed, gradually increasing to high as the whites start to foam. The beating time will vary depending on how many whites you are using so keep a close eye on them. The whites are ready when they reach 'stiff peaks' stage – they should be smooth, moist, shiny and the tips will stand up straight as you lift the beaters out of the bowl.

NOTE: Adding a pinch of cream of tartar or a drop of lemon juice to the mix will help increase volume and stability.

FOLDING WHITES INTO A BATTER

When the whites are beaten to stiff peaks, you need to fold them carefully into your batter right away – as soon as you stop beating they will start to lose air. A metal spoon or rubber spatula is best for doing this. Start by making a well in the centre of your batter or dry ingredients. If it's a wet batter, stir a small spoonful of whites in, just to introduce it to the mix. Now spoon the whites into the centre – use your spatula to cut through the middle, scoop up towards the edge of the bowl and 'fold' back over the top of the whites. Turn the bowl slightly and repeat until all the foam is incorporated. It may look like it's never going to happen, but it will. Just keep folding. Your aim here is to preserve as much of the trapped air as possible while incorporating the foam evenly. Try to handle gently and be patient.

NOTE: Yolks or whole eggs can also be beaten to trap air, but it's only a fraction of what the whites alone will do. When making cakes with whipped egg whites I like to whip up the yolks as well, separately, for extra volume.

CAKE RITUALS

Ever since I started learning about baking I have been obsessed with the history of cake. Its image is so wholesome, unassuming and sweet, yet all around the world its history has mythological, religious, even macabre associations and fantastic stories. It has been assigned magical properties, great symbolism and powers of divination. Cakes have long been tied to ceremonial occasions – we still eat them on significant dates like weddings, birthdays, funerals – but the further back you look through history, the more prominent their role in ritual. Cakes were offered to gods or consumed as part of ceremonies intended to appease them, to encourage good harvests or to ensure the continued rotation of the sun. Here is a collection of just a few cake-related mythologies from around the world.

SOUL CAKES were historically eaten on All Souls' Day. For pagan people, All Souls' Day was the day the dead arose and walked the earth, and they believed they needed to be fed in order to persuade them not to harm the living. The Japanese and Mexicans also make cakes for their dead. People in Germany and Austria would often leave cakes at graves, and the Ancient Egyptians placed them inside tombs.

CHINESE MOON CAKES are still eaten to this day at the Chinese festival for lunar worship. Their symbolism is linked to the mythical Moon Goddess – the Goddess of Immortality, who lives on the moon with a lunar rabbit who makes rice. There is a folk tale that recounts how the overthrow of Mongol rule was once facilitated by messages smuggled in moon cakes, and puzzles printed on their surfaces revealing secret codes that were destroyed when the cakes were eaten.

THE ANCIENT CELTS

rolled cakes down the side of a hill to imitate the sun's rotation and thus ensure it would continue. They also used cakes as a means of divination, even in so far as selecting victims for sacrifice. In a ritual not unlike our tradition of placing a shilling in a Christmas pudding, the Celts would blacken a piece of cake with charcoal; then, when the cake was divided and served, the receiver of the blackened piece would be sacrificed as an offering to the gods. In fact, the Lindow Man – the tar-preserved body of a man killed 2,200 years ago, which currently resides at the British Museum – is thought to have been a victim of just such a ritual. Remnants of his last meal – a partly digested and badly scorched cake – were found in his small intestine.

THE ANCIENT GREEKS left cakes at crossroads to appease Hecate, the testy Goddess of the Underworld. They would leave offerings of 'Hecate cakes' for her, sometimes marked by a single candle so that she could find her way in the dark. This practice is thought by some to be the origin of the tradition of putting birthday candles on cakes. Many cultures made cake offerings to deities, and also offered cakes to the spirits of the dead, believing the cakes would nourish them in the journey to the afterlife.

HINDU TURTLE CAKES are paste cakes of flour shaped like turtles and are made for festivals held in honour of a deity in Taiwanese villages. People buy the cakes at the temple and take them home to assure prosperity, harmony and security.

ULTIMATE PILLOW-SOFT VANILLA SPONGE CAKE

There are lots of variations on the basic vanilla sponge recipe and technique, and this is my favourite. Many hours have been clocked up in the bakery perfecting this recipe, and I can guarantee that this is one of the lightest, most buttery, melt-in-the-mouth vanilla sponge cakes you will find. It's one of the simplest cakes I make, but it's also one of the most popular and I'm constantly asked for the recipe. It is gravity-defyingly light but has a very buttery, almost chewy top. If you perfect one recipe from this book and use it again and again, I would recommend this — simple but delicious, versatile and impressive.

In this recipe all the flour is coated in butter in the initial stage, which inhibits the development of gluten and produces a very soft crumb. There are far fewer air pockets formed by creaming, but this is compensated for with a larger dose of baking powder. As very little gluten is formed to build structure, this is quite a delicate cake, so mind the baking time carefully and be sure to check your oven temperature. Make sure you whisk the dry ingredients together first, as this is a crucial stage for an even result.

PREP TIME

20 minutes

COOKING TIME

30 minutes

SERVES: 8–10

330g plain flour, sifted

320g caster sugar

1 ½ tbsp baking powder

Pinch of salt

175g unsalted butter, room temperature

3 eggs

190ml whole milk

1 ½ tsp good vanilla extract

Two 23cm cake tins, greased and lined,
    or 24 cupcake cases in trays

1   Preheat the oven to 180°C fan assisted/gas mark 6.

2   In a bowl, whisk together the dry ingredients. Beat in the butter until it is incorporated and the mixture appears to be evenly coated and looks like a fine crumble mix – 2–3 minutes on medium speed.

3   Add the eggs and beat, first on medium, then on high, just until incorporated.

4   Add the milk and vanilla and beat, on medium and then on high, until the mixture is smooth and combined; it will appear a bit lighter in colour – 2–3 minutes.

5   Divide the mixture between the two prepared cake tins and level out to the edges. Bake in the oven for 25–30 minutes, or until a toothpick inserted into the centre comes out clean. Remove from the oven and leave to cool in the tins for 10 minutes before turning out onto a wire rack to cool completely.

TIP: Always scrape down the sides of the bowl in between adding ingredients.

SEVEN WAYS WITH VANILLA SPONGE

Once you've perfected the basic vanilla sponge recipe there are dozens of delicious ways it can be adapted and served. Here are some of my favourites.

LAVENDER AND TOASTED ALMOND TEA CAKES

1 batch of Vanilla Sponge, made with Lavender Milk | see page 257 |

1 batch of Lavender Icing
| see page 255 |

2 tsp dried lavender buds, crushed in a pestle and mortar

20g flaked almonds, toasted
| see page 257 |

1 Make up the vanilla sponge, substituting lavender milk for the regular milk, then bake and allow to cool completely.

2 Top each cake with buttercream then dust with the crushed lavender buds and the cooled toasted almonds.

PASSIONFRUIT AND TOASTED ALMOND TEA CAKES

1 batch of Vanilla Sponge

1 batch of Vanilla Buttercream
| see page 254 |

Flesh of 4 passionfruit

40g flaked almonds, toasted
| see page 257 |

1 Make up the vanilla sponge then bake and allow to cool completely.

2 Top each cake with buttercream and a spoonful of passionfruit flesh and finish with toasted almonds.

VANILLA POMEGRANATE LAYER CAKE

1 batch of Vanilla Sponge

1 ripe pomegranate

1 batch of Vanilla Buttercream
| see page 254 |

50g desiccated coconut

1 Make up the vanilla sponge, then bake and allow to cool completely.

2 Seed the pomegranate, making sure all the pith is removed, and use kitchen paper to absorb any excess liquid from the seeds.

3 Use a palette knife or the back of a dessert spoon to spread some of the buttercream on the base layer, to cover. Sprinkle generously with pomegranate seeds and some of the coconut. Sandwich the layers together and repeat for the top layer.

SEVEN WAYS WITH VANILLA SPONGE

LAVENDER AND TOASTED
ALMOND TEA CAKES

COCONUT TEA CAKES

VANILLA COCOA TEA CAKES

VANILLA POMEGRANATE LAYER CAKE

MIXED BERRY VICTORIA SPONGE

PASSIONFRUIT AND TOASTED ALMOND
TEA CAKES

GLITTER CAKE AND COOKIE CANAPÉS

VANILLA COCOA TEA CAKES

I batch of Vanilla Sponge, omitting
    40g of flour | see step I |
40g cocoa, sifted
I batch of Chocolate or Vanilla
    Buttercream
    | see page 254–255 |
Chopped chocolate, toasted nuts or
    desiccated coconut

1 Make up the vanilla sponge, omitting 40g of the flour and folding in the cocoa just before you transfer the batter into the tins. I prefer to do this loosely, so that there are pockets of cocoa sporadically throughout, rather than beating it through evenly, but it's up to you. Bake and allow to cool completely.

2 Top each cake with buttercream and sprinkle with chocolate, nuts or coconut.

COCONUT TEA CAKES

I batch of Vanilla Sponge
50g desiccated coconut
I batch of Vanilla Buttercream
    | see page 254 |
Coconut flakes, toasted on a baking
    sheet in a preheated 180°C fan
    assisted/gas mark 6 oven for
    approximately 4 minutes, or until
    starting to brown

1 Make up the vanilla sponge, folding in 50g of desiccated coconut to the batter. Bake and allow to cool completely.

2 Top each cake with buttercream and dust with the toasted coconut.

MIXED BERRY VICTORIA SPONGE

1 batch of Vanilla Sponge

1 batch of Vanilla Buttercream
    | see page 254 |

1 batch of Mixed Berry Coulis or
    Rhubarb Coulis | see page 256 |

100g fresh summer berries –
    redcurrants, blackcurrants,
    blackberries, strawberries,
    raspberries, gooseberries, in any
    combination, work very well

50g flaked almonds, toasted
    | see page 257 |

1   Make up the vanilla sponge, then bake and allow to cool completely.

2   Spread a thin layer of the buttercream on the base cake layer, drizzle with coulis, and add a smattering of fresh fruit. Sandwich the cakes together and repeat for the top layer, this time using a little more frosting, a drizzle of the coulis, the rest of the fruit and finally the toasted almonds.

GLITTER CAKE AND COOKIE CANAPÉS

1 batch of Vanilla Sponge

Small amount of Vanilla Buttercream
    | see page 254 |

1 batch of Glitter Cookies
    | see page 134 |

1   Make up the vanilla sponge and split the batter between whatever tins you have so that it sits about 1cm deep | re-use the tins and bake in tandem if necessary |.

2   Bake on the middle rack of the preheated oven for 10–15 minutes, or until a toothpick inserted into the centre comes out clean. Allow to cool completely, then use a cookie cutter to cut rounds from the sheet of cake.

3   Assemble by piping a dab of buttercream in the centre of two rounds and sandwiching them as you would a layer cake. Pipe another dab of buttercream on top and top with a glitter cookie. Serve in mini cupcake cases, or just as they are.

    NOTE: Make up a batch of cookies using any recipe you like – gingerbread works well | see page 144 | – then use the method on page 134 to coat them in edible glitter.

BITTER CHOCOLATE ORANGE CAKE

I made a version of this cake for Veuve Clicquot that was huge, many-tiered, painted bright gold and topped with chocolate curls laden with popping candy and candied blood oranges. The sparkling bitter chocolate, orange and popping candy make this cake delicious with champagne, but it's delicious with almost anything.

PREP TIME

20 minutes

COOKING TIME

25 minutes, plus cooling time

SERVES: 10

270g plain flour, sifted

130g caster sugar

1 tsp bicarbonate of soda

Pinch of sea salt

270g dark chocolate
| minimum 70% cocoa solids |
broken into pieces

270g unsalted butter, cubed

270g light brown sugar

Finely grated zest of 1 large orange

4 eggs

100ml natural yoghurt

100ml whole milk

½ batch of Popping Candy Chocolate
Shards | see page 209 |

1 batch of Chocolate Ganache Glaze
| see page 259 |

1 batch of Candied Orange Slices
| see page 226 |

Three 18cm round cake tins,
greased and lined

1 Preheat the oven to 180°C fan assisted/gas mark 6.

2 In a bowl, whisk together the flour, caster sugar, bicarbonate of soda and salt and set aside.

3 Melt the chocolate and butter together in a double boiler | see page XX | over a medium heat. Remove from the heat and allow to cool to room temperature. Beat the chocolate and butter mix into the flour mix, then beat in the brown sugar and orange zest. Now beat in the eggs, one at a time, until just incorporated. Finally, beat in the yoghurt and milk.

4 Divide the mixture between the three prepared cake tins and level out to the edges. Bake for 20–25 minutes, or until a cocktail stick inserted in the centre comes out clean. Remove from the oven and leave to cool in the tins for 10 minutes before turning out onto a wire rack to cool completely.

5 When the cakes are cool, transfer them to a plate one at a time, using a palette knife to spread a thin layer of the ganache glaze between the layers, over the top and all around the edges of the stacked cakes | pour into the centre of the cake, then work down the sides and around the base |. Refrigerate the cake to set the ganache, then repeat the process with a thicker layer of ganache until the cake is evenly covered.

6 Top the finished cake with chocolate shards and orange slices and serve any that remain alongside.

CHERRY AND SEED MADEIRA CAKE

Madeira cake was very popular in the Edwardian era, and I first made this for a project called Salon du Thé, with the theatre company Gideon Reeling. We recreated an Edwardian high tea ceremony – from the food and tea on the menu, to the dress code and interactive performances. This cake made up the centrepiece cutting cake.

PREP TIME

30 minutes

COOKING TIME

30 minutes

SERVES: 8

180g unsalted butter, room
    temperature

180g caster sugar

3 eggs

250g self-raising flour, sifted

3 tbsp milk

75g mixed seeds – pumpkin, sesame,
    poppy

Small handful of fresh pitted cherries
    | about 100g | each sliced into 3
    pieces

Small amount of granulated sugar
    infused with Lapsang Souchong tea
    | optional – see tip |

120ml Mixed Berry Coulis
    | see page 256 | or raspberry jam

150g double cream, whipped

150g icing sugar, sifted

Small amount of lemon juice

Handful of flaked almonds, toasted
    | optional – see page 257 |

Fresh flowers to decorate

Two 18cm round cake tins, greased
    and lined

1   Preheat the oven to 180°C fan assisted/gas mark 6.

2   Cream the butter and sugar together for 4 minutes. Add the eggs, one at a time, and beat until just incorporated. Fold in the flour, then add the milk slowly – you need just enough to ensure that the mixture falls slowly from the spoon. Fold in the seeds and cherries.

3   Divide the mixture between the two prepared cake tins and level out to the edges. Sprinkle the top with some of the Lapsang-infused sugar, if using. Bake for 20–25 minutes, or until a cocktail stick inserted into the centre comes out clean. Remove from the oven and leave to cool in the tins for 10 minutes before turning out onto a wire rack to cool completely.

4   Spread the base layer with the coulis or jam and pipe the whipped cream on top. Sandwich the two halves of the cake together.

5   Mix the icing sugar with enough lemon juice to give it a pouring consistency – or add a dash of coulis, which will also give it a nice pink colour – and pour over the top of the cake. Decorate with toasted almonds and garnish with fresh flowers, if using.

TIP: To infuse granulated sugar with Lapsang Souchong, simply leave an unused tea bag in 400–500g of caster sugar overnight. You can use a small amount for this recipe, then store the rest in an airtight container to use another time.

HOW TO WHIP CREAM

YOU WILL NEED:

A chilled bowl | large enough to hold at
  least double the volume of cream you
  are whipping |
An electric hand whisk
Very cold double cream
1 tsp caster sugar and ¼ tsp vanilla
  extract per 200ml of cream
  | optional |

Pour the cream into the bowl and whip thoroughly and evenly, beginning on a medium speed. Ensure that you run the beaters around the edge of the bowl to keep it all evenly mixed. When the cream starts to thicken and you see the first sign of soft peaks, add the sugar and the vanilla, if using. Now reduce the speed to medium-low and watch carefully – it's almost done. Continue just until you have very soft peaks. Using an electric hand mixer this should take under 2 minutes.

ZEBRA CAKE

This is a version of the 'rainbow cake' recipe that appeared in my last book, but uses the classic combination of chocolate and vanilla sponge. It looks amazing when it's cut into — the striped effect is made with two separate batters that are layered on top of each other in the tin before they go into the oven.

PREP TIME

25 minutes

COOKING TIME

30 minutes

SERVES: 8

260g unsalted butter, room
    temperature

420g caster sugar

4 eggs

430g plain flour, sifted

1 tbsp baking powder

Pinch of salt

1 tsp vanilla extract

240ml whole milk

30g cocoa powder, sifted

1 batch of Chocolate or Vanilla
    Buttercream | see pages 254–255 |

Three 15cm round cake tins, greased
    and lined

1   Preheat the oven to 180°C fan assisted/gas mark 6.

2   Beat the butter and sugar together until light and fluffy — approximately 4 minutes. Add the eggs and beat slowly at first, then on medium, until just evenly incorporated, scraping down the bowl after each stage. Remove half the batter and set aside.

3   In another bowl, whisk together half the flour, baking powder and salt. Add half these dry ingredients to the batter | so a quarter of the total | and beat on medium speed until incorporated. Add the vanilla and half the milk, then the rest of the dry ingredients. This is your vanilla batter. Set aside.

4   Now clean and dry your mixing bowl and put in the second half of the batter.

5   In your second bowl, whisk the remaining flour, baking powder and salt with the cocoa powder. Repeat the process, adding half the dry ingredients to the batter, then the milk, then the remaining dry ingredients, making sure you scrape down the bowl with each addition and be careful not to over-beat. This is your chocolate batter.

6   To make the zebra stripes, spoon about 3 tablespoons of the vanilla batter into the centre of each of your prepared cake tins. Then add 3 tablespoons of the chocolate batter into the centre of that. The vanilla batter will spread out. Continue alternating the batters, adding to the centre each time. Once you are done, don't be tempted to level the top or merge the layers in any way!

7   Bake for approximately 25–30 minutes, or until a cocktail stick inserted into the centre comes out clean | or just with a few crumbs, and no liquid |. Remove from the oven and leave to cool in the tins for 10 minutes before turning out onto a wire rack to cool completely.

8   Spread buttercream on both layers, sandwich together, and spread more buttercream around the sides.

BEETROOT CAKE

I first made this cake for someone who had food intolerances that meant they could hardly ever eat cake. It's virtually savoury and contains no butter or flour, but still has a beautiful colour, texture and flavour. The original version had no added sugar, but I've adapted it slightly with honey and brown sugar to complement the natural sweetness of the beetroot. This cake is delicious with the mascarpone frosting on its own, or you could add some icing sugar to it if you like. Warning: this is a cake for grown-ups.

PREP TIME

40 minutes

COOKING TIME

30 minutes

SERVES: 8–10

500g raw beetroots, peeled and grated
   very fine

120ml olive oil

60ml freshly squeezed smooth orange juice

80g root ginger, peeled and finely grated

150g raisins

6 tbsp runny honey

1½ tsp vanilla extract

Finely grated zest of 2 lemons

½ tsp ground cinnamon

1 tsp freshly grated nutmeg

2 tsp baking powder

360g polenta | instant coarse polenta will do |

4 eggs, separated

50g light brown sugar

Fresh fruit, such as berries or sliced
   peaches, to decorate

Handful of chives, chopped

FOR THE FROSTING

400g mascarpone

A dash of beetroot juice to colour
   | optional |

100g icing sugar, sifted | optional |

Two 18cm round cake tins, greased and lined

1   Preheat the oven to 180°C fan assisted/gas mark 6.

2   Combine the beetroot, oil, juice, ginger, raisins, honey, vanilla, lemon zest and spices in a bowl. Put the baking powder and polenta in a separate bowl and stir to combine.

3   Beat the egg yolks with the brown sugar until creamy and increased in volume – approximately 4 minutes. Stir into the beetroot mix.

4   In a clean bowl, whisk the egg whites until stiff peaks form | see page 35 for how |. Stir the polenta evenly into the beetroot mix, then fold in the egg whites | see page 35 |.

5   Divide the mixture between the two prepared cake tins and level out to the edges. Bake for 30–35 minutes, or until a cocktail stick inserted into the centre comes out clean. Remove from the oven and leave to cool in the tins for 10 minutes before turning out onto a wire rack to cool completely.

6   Beat the beetroot juice and icing sugar into the mascarpone, if using. Spread the cake rounds with the frosting, then add the fruit, sandwich together and sprinkle with the chopped chives.

TIP: If possible, use a food processor with a fine grating attachment to grate the beetroot – you can do it by hand, but it's hard work, and be prepared for stained hands.

FLOURLESS OREO CAKE

This cake came about when a customer called to order a gluten-free Oreo cake. A slight language barrier coupled with a crackly line meant I couldn't explain that Oreos themselves contained gluten. In the end I gave up and conceded, went to the kitchen and made this cake — the cocoa powder combined with the dark colour and crunch of the poppy seeds make for a convincing Oreo texture and flavour, especially when married with a dollop of vanilla buttercream. This recipe works well for a dozen fairy cakes too.

PREP TIME

25 minutes

COOKING TIME

30 minutes

SERVES: 8

130g unsalted butter, room temperature

140g light brown sugar

4 eggs, separated

150g black/blue poppy seeds

130g ground almonds

40g cocoa powder, sifted

Pinch of salt

1 tsp baking powder

300g batch Vanilla Buttercream
| see page 254 |

20g dark chocolate, roughly chopped
| optional |

One 23cm round cake tin, greased and lined

1   Preheat the oven to 180°C fan assisted/gas mark 6.

2   Beat together the butter and sugar until light and fluffy — approximately 4 minutes. Add the egg yolks gradually and mix until combined.

3   Mix together the poppy seeds, ground almonds, cocoa, salt and baking powder in a separate bowl.

4   Beat the egg whites in a very clean bowl, first on slow, then on medium and finally on high, until they form stiff peaks | see page 35|.

5   By hand, stir half the poppy seed mix into the batter, then fold in half the beaten egg whites, the rest of the poppy seed mix and finally the remaining egg whites. Use the folding technique to incorporate everything | see page 35 |, adding very gently with a metal spoon or spatula and taking care not to knock too much air out of the egg whites. Don't worry if there are still white streaks or lumps — just try to fold in so that everything is roughly evenly distributed.

6   Transfer the mixture to your prepared tin and level out to the edges. Bake for 25–30 minutes, until risen and firm. Press the top of the cake gently with your fingertips to see if it feels baked through. Remove from the oven and leave to cool in the tin for 10 minutes before turning out onto a wire rack to cool completely.

7   When cool, spread the buttercream on top and dust with roughly chopped dark chocolate, if desired.

SUMMER CARROT CAKE

Feel free to change the spices and fruit as the seasons change. Summer is citrussy, with passionfruit and light cream cheese frosting.

PREP TIME
30 minutes
COOKING TIME
20 minutes
SERVES: 8

175ml runny honey

75ml water

120ml thick mango or citrus smoothie

125g unsalted butter

250g peeled and trimmed organic
    carrots, grated

90g raisins or stoned and chopped
    dates, or a mix of both

Flesh of 2 passionfruit

Juice and finely grated zest of 1 orange

Pinch of cinnamon

225g wholegrain spelt flour, sifted

2 tsp bicarbonate of soda

100g nuts | walnuts and pecans are good |
    toasted | see page 257 |, then broken
    into pieces

½ batch of Cream Cheese Frosting
    | see page 255 |

50g flaked almonds, toasted, for
    topping

Flesh of 2 passionfruit

Sprinkling of desiccated coconut

Two 18cm round cake tins, greased
    and lined

1 Preheat the oven to
   180°C fan assisted/
   gas mark 6.

2 Heat the honey, water,
   smoothie or brandy,
   butter, carrot mix, dried
   and fresh fruit, citrus zest
   and juice, and spices together
   in a pan, stirring gently to melt
   the butter. Bring to the boil, then
   boil for 6 minutes. Take the mixture
   off the heat, remove the cloves if using,
   and allow to cool completely to room
   temperature – transfer to another bowl to
   speed up this process.

3 Meanwhile, in a bowl whisk together the
   flour and bicarbonate of soda and stir in the
   crushed nuts.

WINTER CARROT CAKE

Winter is lots of nutmeg, cardamom, brandy and dried fruit.

PREP TIME
30 minutes
COOKING TIME
20 minutes
SERVES: 8

175ml runny honey

75ml water

120ml brandy

125g unsalted butter

250g any combination of carrots, parsnips, beetroots or sweet potatoes, grated

90g raisins or stoned and chopped dates, or a mix of both

Juice and finely grated zest of 1 orange

Pinch of cinnamon

¼ nutmeg, finely grated

Seeds from 4 cardamom pods, crushed

4 cloves

225g wholegrain spelt flour, sifted

2 tsp bicarbonate of soda

100g nuts | walnuts and pecans are good | toasted | see page 257 |, then broken into pieces

½ batch of Cream Cheese Frosting | see page 255 |

Extra nuts, toasted, for topping

Beetroot crisps | see page 71 |

Two 18cm round cake tins, greased and lined

4 Fold the wet mix into the dry. Divide the mixture between the two prepared cake tins and level out to the edges. Bake for 20 minutes, or until golden brown and a toothpick comes out clean. Remove from the oven and leave to cool in the tins for 10 minutes before turning out onto a wire rack to cool completely.

5 Sandwich the cake layers together with cream cheese frosting | add a teaspoon of brandy for the winter version |, spread a layer on top, and sprinkle with the toasted nuts and any other toppings you are using.

APPLE AND ROSEMARY OLIVE OIL CAKE

This is a perfect daytime cake; it's very moist and has a lovely depth of flavour with the spices, brown sugar, apples and rosemary. It's usually best a day or two after making — when the spices and flavours really come through. Delicious served warm with vanilla ice cream | see page 241 | or at room temperature with coffee.

Baking with olive oil has been done for centuries and is very common in Mediterranean cooking. It gives baked goods a light texture and can often be used as a substitute for butter or other oils. It's best to use a lower-intensity extra virgin olive oil for a subtle flavour.

PREP TIME

20 minutes

COOKING TIME

35 minutes

SERVES: 8

190g plain white flour

⅓ tsp freshly grated nutmeg

⅓ tsp ground cinnamon

1 tsp baking powder

85g unsalted butter, room temperature

85g dark brown sugar, plus extra for dusting

2 eggs

1½ tbsp olive oil

240g peeled and cored Bramley cooking apples, very finely diced

½ tsp fresh rosemary leaves, finely chopped

2–3 Bramley apple slices

2 fresh rosemary sprigs to decorate

One 23cm round cake tin, greased and lined

1 Preheat the oven to 180°C fan assisted/gas mark 6.

2 Whisk together the flour, spices and baking powder to ensure they are evenly mixed. Set aside.

3 Beat the butter and sugar together until light and fluffy — approximately 4 minutes. Beat in the eggs, then add the oil and beat to incorporate. Mix in the diced apple and chopped rosemary, then fold in the dry ingredients.

4 Transfer into the prepared cake tin, level the edges and lay the slices of apple on top. Coat the surface of the cake with a thin layer of brown sugar. Dip the sprigs of rosemary into cold water, dust with brown sugar, then press onto the top of the cake.

5 Bake for 30–35 minutes, or until firm in the centre and a cocktail stick inserted comes out clean. Remove from the oven and leave to cool in the tin for 10 minutes before turning out onto a wire rack to cool completely, or serve warm.

CHOCOLATE AVOCADO CAKE

This is a rich, moist, very chocolaty cake. Avocado replaces butter as the fat in the icing here, not to make it a healthy cake but for the beautiful flavour and creamy texture. Topped with toasted walnuts and dark chocolate shavings, this cake has a beautiful, slightly unusual flavour and the added bonus of some healthy fats.

PREP TIME

30 minutes

COOKING TIME

25 minutes

SERVES: 8

200g dark chocolate

| minimum 70% cocoa solids |

broken into pieces

1 tsp espresso powder

200g plain flour, sifted

2 tsp bicarbonate of soda

Pinch of salt

200g unsalted butter, room
temperature

200g dark brown sugar

4 large eggs

100ml natural yoghurt

FOR THE TOPPING

Flesh of 1 ripe Hass avocado, brown
bits discarded | 150g flesh |

¾ tsp lemon juice

250g icing sugar, sifted

Extra chocolate for dusting, shaved
with a zester

30g walnuts, toasted | see page 257 |

Two 18cm round cake tins, greased
and lined

1   Preheat the oven to 180°C fan assisted/gas mark 6.

2   Melt the chocolate gently in a double boiler with the espresso powder. Remove from the heat and allow to cool. Whisk together the flour, bicarbonate of soda and salt in a bowl and set aside.

3   Beat the butter and sugar until light and fluffy – approximately 4 minutes. Beat in the eggs one at a time, beating just enough to incorporate each one. Beat in half the flour mix, then the yoghurt, then the remaining flour. Finally add the cooled melted chocolate, until just evenly combined.

4   Divide the mixture between the two prepared cake tins and level out to the edges. Bake for 20–25 minutes, or until a cocktail stick comes out clean. Remove from the oven and leave to cool in the tins for 10 minutes before turning out onto a wire rack to cool completely.

5   Meanwhile make the topping. Using a food processor, blend the avocado with the lemon juice until you achieve a smooth texture, working out any lumps. Slowly blend in the icing sugar, increasing the speed of the mixer as you go | feel free to add more or less sugar to achieve a consistency and taste you like |. The consistency of the frosting will vary greatly depending on the ripeness of the avocado you use, so you will have to keep tasting and testing until you get a consistency and flavour you are happy with. If it's still very runny and you don't want to add more sugar, you can transfer it to the fridge to firm up.

6   Spread the topping over the cooled cakes. Sprinkle with the chocolate shavings and top with the cooled toasted walnuts.

MARGARITA DRIZZLE CAKE

I'm a huge margarita fan, so it was only a matter of time before it ended up in cake form.
This cake is best served soon after making.

PREP TIME

35 minutes

COOKING TIME

30 minutes

SERVES: 8–10

450g plain flour, sifted

1 tbsp baking powder

½ tsp salt

120g unsalted butter, room
 temperature

300g caster sugar

Finely grated zest of 2 limes

4 large eggs

300ml whole milk

1 batch of Candied Lime Slices
 | see page 226 | with 50ml tequila
 added to the pan with the limes

FOR THE SYRUP

225ml water

375g caster sugar

300ml tequila

Juice of 5 limes | approximately 100ml |

Three 18cm round cake tins, greased
 and lined

1 Preheat the oven to 180°C fan assisted/gas mark 6.

2 Whisk together the flour, baking powder and salt and set aside.

3 Beat the butter and sugar until light and fluffy – approximately 4 minutes. Beat in the lime zest briefly. Then add the eggs gradually, beating just to incorporate. If the mixture starts to split you can add a spoonful of flour to bring it back together. Now add half the dry mixture and beat to combine, then the milk, then the remaining dry. Beat all together for 1–2 minutes.

4 Divide the mixture between the three prepared cake tins and level out to the edges. Bake for 25–30 minutes, or until firm to the touch and a cocktail stick inserted in the centre comes out clean. Remove from the oven, leave to cool in the tins for 10 minutes, then turn out onto a wire rack placed over a baking tray and prick each cake all over with a cocktail stick.

5 Meanwhile make the syrup. Heat the water, sugar, 150ml of the tequila and the lime juice in a medium-sized heavy-bottomed pan over a high heat, stirring continuously, for 15 minutes, until you have a thickening syrup that is just starting to colour. Turn up the heat briefly so the mixture bubbles up before turning off. Pour in the remaining tequila.

6 While the syrup is still hot | but not boiling | drizzle it all over each warm cake | the baking tray will catch the excess syrup |, making sure you cover all sides and keeping some back to serve with the cake. Let the cakes soak up the syrup, then drizzle any excess over again.

7 When cool, stack the cakes one on top of the other, top with the candied limes and serve with a fresh drizzle of syrup with each slice.

PORTER CAKE

Our bakery is just up the road from the Truman Brewery, the birthplace of porter – named for its popularity at the time with London's street and river porters. It was used a lot in Victorian baking, as the alcohol preserves the cake and gives it a deep, rich flavour. Over the years, porter fell out of popularity, but it has been having a bit of a revival lately and some good new ones are available. If you can't get hold of any porter, you can substitute Guinness.

PREP TIME

45 minutes

COOKING TIME

45 minutes

SERVES: 8

230g unsalted butter, cubed

290g mixed dried fruit

| raisins, sultanas, stoned and chopped dates |

Juice and finely grated zest of 1 orange

160g dark brown sugar

280ml porter

2 eggs

2 egg yolks

260g plain flour, sifted

½ tsp freshly grated nutmeg

1 tsp mixed spice

1 tsp baking powder

60g flaked almonds

FOR THE PORTER SYRUP

150ml porter

100g dark brown sugar

One 20 x 12cm loaf tin, 8cm deep, greased and lined

1 Preheat the oven to 160°C fan assisted/gas mark 4.

2 Put the butter, dried fruit, orange juice and zest, sugar and porter into a heavy-bottomed pan over a medium heat and slowly bring to the boil, stirring gently until the butter melts and the sugar liquefies. Turn the heat down low and simmer for around 15 minutes, then remove from the heat and allow to cool for another 15 minutes.

3 Beat the eggs and egg yolks together lightly and stir into the pan. In a bowl, whisk together the flour, spices and baking powder before adding them to the pan, stirring to bring it all together evenly.

4 Transfer the batter into the prepared tin, level to the edges and sprinkle with the almonds. Bake for 40–50 minutes, or until a skewer inserted into the centre comes out clean. Remove from the oven and leave the cake to cool in the tin for 15 minutes, then carefully pull it out of the tin and place it still in the paper on a wire rack to cool completely.

5 Meanwhile make the syrup. Heat the porter and sugar in a medium heavy-bottomed pan on a low heat until the sugar has dissolved, then bring to the boil and simmer vigorously for 6–7 minutes, or until glossy and thickened.

6 Pierce the cake all over with a cocktail stick, then use a pastry brush to cover the entire cake in the still hot syrup, brushing extra into the holes.

SIMPLE DECADENT CHOCOLATE CAKE

This recipe has been with me for years — it's a simple, reliable recipe that's very rich and indulgent. It's lovely with vanilla or chocolate icing and fresh fruit or nuts. If you ever accidentally end up with one that's slightly underdone, fresh from the oven and no one's looking, make sure you eat it immediately with vanilla ice cream | see page 241 | or double cream.

PREP TIME

25 minutes

COOKING TIME

35 minutes

SERVES: 8-10

230g unsalted butter, room
   temperature

550g caster sugar

4 eggs

2 tsp vanilla extract

420g plain flour, sifted

90g cocoa powder, sifted

1 tsp salt

1 tsp bicarbonate of soda

380ml soured cream

250ml strong brewed coffee, cooled

1 batch of Chocolate or Vanilla
   Buttercream | see pages 254–255 |

Small amount of dark chocolate,
   chopped and toasted nuts, or fresh
   berries and desiccated coconut,
   to decorate

Two 23cm round cake tins, greased
   and lined

1   Preheat the oven to 180°C fan assisted/gas mark 6.

2   Cream together the butter and sugar until very light and fluffy — approximately 4 minutes. Then add the eggs and vanilla and beat on a slow speed, gradually increasing until just evenly incorporated.

3   Whisk together all the dry ingredients in a bowl. Add half to the batter, then the soured cream, then the remaining dry ingredients, keeping beating to a minimum.

4   Once you have a smooth even batter, gradually add the coffee. The mixture will be very wet, so beat slowly to incorporate.

5   Divide the mixture between the two prepared cake tins and level out to the edges. Bake for 30–35 minutes, or until a cocktail stick inserted in the centre comes out clean. Remove from the oven and leave to cool in the tins for 10 minutes before turning out onto a wire rack to cool completely.

6   Spread the buttercream on the base layer, sandwich the cakes together and spread more buttercream on top. If you're using chocolate buttercream, sprinkle with chopped dark chocolate and toasted nuts; if you're using vanilla, top with desiccated coconut and fresh berries.

TIP: If you can't get hold of soured cream you can substitute full-fat natural yoghurt.

PEAR, PARSNIP AND GINGER CAKE

Root vegetables are often overlooked in cake making. Beetroot, parsnip and sweet potato all have a lovely texture when baked, and as much natural sweetness as carrots. Parsnips have a subtle butteriness, and combined with pear and ginger make a beautiful cake, moist and rich in flavour, with the parsnip like a spice note in the background. The pear crisps require a bit of planning, so bake these in advance if using. This cake is at its best the day after baking, when all the flavours have come through.

PREP TIME

30 minutes

COOKING TIME

1 ½ hours

SERVES: 8

250g peeled and cored mixed pears and parsnips, grated

100g raisins

20g fresh ginger, peeled and finely grated

Juice and finely grated zest of 1 lemon

150g plain, wholemeal or wholegrain spelt flour, sifted

¾ tsp freshly grated nutmeg, to taste

1 tsp baking powder

150g ground almonds or hazelnuts

3 eggs

150g light brown sugar, plus extra for topping

125ml olive oil

½ batch of Cream Cheese Frosting
| see page 255 |

50g hazelnuts, toasted | see page 257 | then roughly chopped

One 23cm round cake tin, greased and lined

1   Preheat the oven to 180°C fan assisted/ gas mark 6.

2   Use kitchen paper to soak up any excess moisture from the grated fruit and vegetables, then put them into a bowl with the raisins, ginger, lemon juice and zest, and combine.

3   In another bowl, whisk together the flour, nutmeg, baking powder and ground almonds/hazelnuts. Set aside.

4   Beat the eggs and sugar until very light and airy – approximately 5 minutes on high speed – then add the oil, beating to incorporate. Beat for another 2 minutes before folding in first the flour mix, then the pear and parsnip mix. Transfer the mixture to your prepared cake tin and level out to the edges.

5   Bake for 30 minutes, or until risen and a cocktail stick inserted into the centre comes out with no more than a few sticky crumbs. Remove from the oven and leave to cool in the tin for 10 minutes before turning out onto a wire rack to cool completely.

6   Spread the cream cheese frosting over the top of the cooled cake, then top with the chopped roasted hazelnuts and the pear crisps.

FOR THE PEAR CRISPS

120ml water

1 tbsp caster sugar

A squeeze of lemon juice

1 large reasonably firm pear, cored and
   finely sliced

One baking tray, greased and lined

Preheat the oven to 110°C fan assisted/gas mark ½. Bring the water to the boil in a heavy-bottomed pan with the sugar and lemon juice. Turn off the heat and stir until the sugar has dissolved. Dip the pear slices into the sugar water, transfer to the lined baking tray, and bake for 30 minutes to 1 hour, or until dried out. Try to resist eating them all before you decorate your cake. Try making crisps with other fruit and vegetables, just remember to adjust the baking time accordingly.

RED VELVET

Red velvet is a traditional Southern American recipe that has long been 'America's favourite cake'. The red sponge originated from the acidity in natural cocoa powder and buttermilk reacting with bicarbonate of soda and creating a reddish tinge – this is probably where devil's food cake got its name too. While most recipes call for food colouring in order to achieve a startling deep red, some people use beetroot juice for a more natural colouring. However you colour it (or don't) this is a beautifully dense, rich cake with a subtle hint of chocolate that's not too sweet.

PREP TIME

40 minutes

COOKING TIME

25 minutes

SERVES: 8

115g unsalted butter, room
  temperature

280g caster sugar

2 eggs

1½ tbsp red liquid food colouring
  | Dr Oetker works well |

325g plain flour, sifted

30g cocoa powder, sifted

250ml buttermilk

1 tsp bicarbonate of soda

1 tsp cider vinegar

Two 18cm round cake tins, greased and
  lined, or 15 cupcake cases in a tray

1   Preheat the oven to 180°C fan assisted/gas mark 6.

2   Cream together the butter and sugar until light and fluffy, starting on medium and increasing to high speed – the mixture should be pale and increased in volume, about 4 minutes. Add the eggs gradually, then the food colouring, and beat until just incorporated.

3   Sift together the flour and cocoa and add half to the batter, beating to incorporate evenly and ensuring you scrape down the sides. Then beat in the buttermilk and finally the second half of the dry ingredients.

4   In a small bowl, using a clean spatula or teaspoon, mix together the bicarbonate of soda and cider vinegar | it will fizz up | and fold it immediately into the batter – do not use the mixer, just fold evenly with a spatula by hand.

5   Divide the mixture between the two prepared cake tins and level out to the edges. Bake for 20–25 minutes, or until a toothpick inserted into the centre comes out clean. Remove from the oven and leave to cool in the tins for 10 minutes before turning out onto a wire rack to cool completely.

TIP: If you are stuck for buttermilk you can make a decent substitute by adding 1 teaspoon of lemon juice to every 250ml of whole milk – just make sure you re-measure it before adding it to a batter.

MINI LAYER CAKE CANAPÉS

1 Make up a batch of the red velvet batter | see page 72 |. Split it between whatever tins you have so that it sits about 1cm deep | re-use the tins and bake in tandem if necessary |. Bake in the middle of the preheated oven at 180°C fan assisted/gas mark 6 for 15 minutes, or until a toothpick inserted in the centre comes out clean.

2 Allow to cool completely, then use a 5cm cookie cutter | or any other size you like | to cut rounds from the sheet of cake.

3 Assemble by piping a dab of cream cheese frosting | tinted with a drop of red food colouring if you like | in the centre of two rounds and sandwich them together like you would a layer cake. Pipe another dab on top and finish with a berry, a shard of chocolate | see page 209 |, toasted nuts or whatever you like.

RED VELVET LAYER CAKE

Make up a batch of red velvet cake | see page 72 |. Make up a batch of cream cheese frosting | see page 255 | and spread it between the two layers and on top. Decorate however you like – try using a small handful of desiccated coconut, fresh red berries, flaked almonds or roughly chopped dark chocolate.

BLEEDING HEARTS

I first made these hearts for my last book – a zombie-themed, B-movie-inspired cake-decorating book – and they exploded on Valentine's Day. Inundated with orders from all over the world, I made hundreds of the little bleeders, but since I couldn't ship them outside London I shared the recipe on my blog. They are actually very simple to make; just find an image that you want to copy and keep it in front of you while you work with the fondant.

I cooled batch of Red Velvet cupcakes
| see page 72 |

75g red fondant icing per cupcake

Small amount of Vanilla Buttercream
| see page 254 | or Cream Cheese
Frosting | see page 255 |

A tub of clear piping gel | clear gel used
for decorating cakes, which gives a glossy
finish |

Red food colouring | optional black, too –
important: use a gel colouring, not a liquid |

I batch of Mixed Berry Coulis
| see page 256 |

1   For each bleeding heart, take 75g of fondant icing and roll it into an oval shape about 0.5cm thick, roughly 20 x 10cm | a small silicone rolling pin and mat will help to stop it sticking, otherwise use icing sugar |. Place one of the cupcakes in the centre of the oval and pipe a little bit of buttercream or frosting to stick it in place. Wrap the fondant around the cake from both the edges, folding inwards to the front of the cake, then fold in the bottom, cutting away any excess, and use the extra fondant at the top to form the arteries. Don't worry about any creases or gathering in the fondant – they make for useful gory details later on.

2   In a small bowl, mix a spoonful of the clear piping gel with some drops of red | and black, if you like | food colouring. Now paint the fondant heart all over using a soft brush – it will stay really glossy.

3   When you are ready to serve, use a pipette or spoon to add coulis 'blood' to the arteries, and in a puddle around the base, and prepare to eat your heart out.

FLOURLESS CHOCOLATE
AFTER DINNER CAKE

This is a classic simple dessert, a good one to practise and perfect for showing off at dinner parties. I have made many variations of this cake and this recipe is by far my favourite. If you want an even simpler, quicker, foolproof dessert, you can simply beat in the eggs whole. If you don't want to use the cacao nibs, try pistachio nuts instead, or dust the finished cake with cocoa or icing sugar. It's delicious served hot or cold with ice cream, double cream or fresh berries.

PREP TIME

25 minutes

COOKING TIME

25 minutes

SERVES: 8-10

300g dark chocolate

| minimum 70% cocoa solids |

broken into pieces

1 tsp espresso powder | optional |

200g unsalted butter, cubed

6 eggs, separated

100g brown sugar, preferably dark

½ tsp vanilla extract

Good pinch of sea salt

1 tsp baking powder

5 tbsp cocoa powder, sifted

Handful of cacao nibs | optional |

One 23cm round cake tin, greased
and lined

1   Preheat the oven to 180°C fan assisted/gas mark 6.

2   In a double boiler | see page 196 |, melt together the chocolate, espresso powder and butter, then remove from the heat and set aside.

3   In a large bowl, whisk together the egg yolks and sugar on high for 5 minutes until yellow and creamy, then add the vanilla and salt.

4   In a clean, dry bowl beat the egg whites and the baking powder together, starting on a low speed and increasing the speed gently until stiff peaks are formed | see page 35 |.

5   Stir the chocolate mixture into the yolk mixture, then stir in the cocoa. Now stir in a small spoonful of the beaten whites. Once that's mixed through, carefully fold in the remaining whites in two parts, until just incorporated | see page 35 for tips on how to fold in whites |.

6   Transfer to your prepared tin, level out to the edges and sprinkle the cacao nibs on top of the batter, if using. Bake for approximately 25 minutes – the middle should wobble slightly when the tin is shaken gently, like a brownie. Remove from the oven and leave to cool in the tin for 10 minutes before turning out onto a wire rack to cool completely, or serve hot.

HAZELNUT AND PINEAPPLE
UPSIDE-DOWN CAKE

Pineapple upside-down cake is one of those unfortunate desserts that was put through the wringer in post-war Britain, being repeatedly made with tinned fruit, glacé cherries and basic recipes. This version adds some nuts and spice and coconut and brings it back to life with fresh fruit and a moist cake. If you prefer a more pudding-like upside-down cake, you can bake this cake in a 2-litre metal bowl. Just double the quantities and follow the method below.

PREP TIME

25 minutes

COOKING TIME

55 minutes

SERVES: 8

30g light brown sugar, for dusting

1 medium pineapple, peeled and sliced
    to 4mm thickness | about 200g fruit |

200g unsalted butter, room
    temperature

150g caster sugar

4 eggs, separated

4 tbsp pineapple juice

160g wholegrain spelt flour, sifted

Good pinch of salt

½ tsp baking powder

3 tbsp desiccated coconut

1 tsp freshly grated nutmeg

½ tsp ground mixed spice

150g blanched hazelnuts, ground for
    30 seconds in a food processor

Fresh cherries, desiccated coconut
    or chopped roasted hazelnuts, to
    decorate

One 23cm round cake tin, 5–8cm deep,
    greased | NOT loose-bottomed |

1 Preheat the oven to 160°C fan assisted/gas mark 4.

2 Sprinkle the bottom of your well-greased tin with brown sugar and cover with the slices of pineapple.

3 Beat the butter and sugar together until light and fluffy — approximately 4 minutes. Gradually beat in the egg yolks and 3 tablespoons of the juice, followed by the flour, salt, baking powder, desiccated coconut, spices and ground hazelnuts. Then add the remaining juice.

4 In a clean bowl whisk the egg whites until stiff peaks form | see page 35 |. Gently fold the egg whites into the batter, one third at a time | see page 35 |.

5 Transfer to your prepared cake tin, level out to the edges and bake for 35–45 minutes, or until a cocktail stick inserted into the centre comes out clean. NOTE: If you are making this in the 2-litre bowl, you will need to bake it for longer. If the batter is starting to brown at the top but needs more baking time, you can cover it with a baking sheet or a piece of tin foil.

6 Remove from the oven and leave to cool in the tin completely before carefully turning out onto a plate. Sprinkle with desiccated coconut, fresh cherries or roughly chopped toasted hazelnuts.

GLUTEN-FREE CARROT AND COURGETTE CAKE

A lovely cake for the summer, again using vegetables for moisture and a fresh texture and flavour. Experiment with adding different seeds, zests, nuts and spices.

PREP TIME

40 minutes

COOKING TIME

40 minutes

SERVES: 8–10

400g peeled and trimmed mixed carrots and courgettes, grated

90g sultanas

100ml orange juice | if you squeeze your own, add the finely grated zest of the fruit too |

6 eggs

300g caster sugar

250ml olive oil

500g blanched hazelnuts, ground for 30 seconds in a food processor | or ground almonds |

1 tsp baking powder

1 tsp grated fresh nutmeg

½ tsp ground cinnamon

2 tbsp desiccated coconut

60g sunflower and pumpkin seeds, plus extra for dusting

1 batch of Cream Cheese Frosting | see page 255 |

Two 23cm round cake tins, greased with olive oil

1   Preheat the oven to 180°C fan assisted/gas mark 6.

2   Use kitchen paper to soak up any excess moisture from the grated vegetables, then put them into a bowl, add the sultanas and orange juice and leave to soak.

3   Whisk together the eggs and sugar until light and airy – approximately 7 minutes. Slowly add the olive oil in a steady stream, beating just enough to incorporate completely.

4   Whisk together the ground hazelnuts and the baking powder, and fold in with the orange zest | if using |, spices and coconut. Finally fold in the soaked carrots, courgettes and sultanas, and the seeds.

5   Divide the mixture evenly between the two prepared cake tins and level out to the edges. Bake for 30–40 minutes, or until the top has risen and a cocktail stick inserted into the centre comes out crumby but clean. Remove from the oven and allow to cool in the tins for 10 minutes before turning out onto a wire rack to cool completely.

6   When cool, spread the base layer with cream cheese frosting, sandwich together and spread more frosting on the top. Sprinkle with more sunflower and pumpkin seeds.

VERY BOOZY SHERRY TRIFLE

I made this trifle for a supper club called 'The English Laundrette' – a cheeky spin on the French Laundry. The menu reworked 1960s English fare, brought up to date by ever-inspiring chef Carl Clarke. We made the puds and featured mini versions of our Bakewells | see page 102 | and our hazelnut and pineapple upside-down cake | see page 81 |.

PREP TIME

1 hour 10 minutes

COOKING TIME

1 hour 15 minutes

SERVES: 12

200ml medium sweet sherry

3 batches of Mixed Berry Coulis
| see page 256 |

1 batch of Vanilla Sponge
| see page 38 | cooled and preferably a few days old

2 batches of Basic Egg Custard
| see page 260 |

350g mixed fresh berries – chopped strawberries, blueberries, raspberries, stoned and chopped cherries, redcurrants

½ batch of Oaty Crumble
| see page 128 |, cooled | optional |

50g flaked almonds, toasted
| see page 257 |

One large glass bowl,
around 5 litres capacity

1 In a bowl, stir together the sherry and coulis.

2 Place half of one layer of cake in the bottom of your glass bowl. Ladle a layer of custard on top, sprinkle with fresh berries and drizzle with some of the coulis mix. Repeat to the top!

3 Finish with a layer of fruit, top with the oaty crumble if using, and serve dusted with the cooled toasted flaked almonds.

CRUMBLE

COULIS

BERRIES

CUSTARD

SPONGE

DECORATING CAKES

This chapter shares some ideas for decorating the cakes in this book. Feel free to use the methods and techniques to decorate cakes in your own style. Cake decorators sculpt beautiful designs with sugar paste and fondant but it feels like cheating – I try to decorate with things that taste as good as they look.

ROSES CAKE

Choose a cake you want to make – I used the summer/winter carrot cake recipe on page 58. Cool the cakes completely, then fit a piping bag with a 1M tip and fill with a frosting of your choice | I used the vanilla buttercream on page 254 and coloured it with fresh raspberries | – it should be firm enough to hold its shape. Brush up your piping bag skills by reading the tips on page 26, then pipe some frosting between the two cake layers and use a palette knife or the back of a spoon to spread it evenly. Once the layers are stacked, start from the centre of the cake and pipe clockwise in a spiral, starting from the centre and working your way out to make a rose. Repeat, piping roses in different sizes to cover the cake.

CAKE WITH EDIBLE FLOWERS

Choose a cake you want to make – I used the red velvet cake recipe on page 72. Make up some crystallised flowers | see page 230 | and a batch of frosting of your choice | I used the cream cheese frosting on page 255 |. When the cakes are completely cool, use a palette knife to spread the frosting between the layers as you stack them up. Decorate the cake however you like – I rough-chopped a 200g bar of dark chocolate and used it to sprinkle around the sides of the cake. Then arrange your crystallised flowers on top.

CHOCOLATE DECORATED CAKE

Choose a cake you want to make – I used the bitter chocolate orange cake recipe on page 46. Make up a batch of frosting of your choice | I used the chocolate buttercream recipe on page 255 |. Make up a double batch of the chocolate shards on page 209, using cellophane rather than baking paper. Don't roll them up but leave in sheets to cool. Cut one sheet into strips lengthways, 7cm apart. Then cut these strips widthways at 10cm intervals. Cut up the second sheet more haphazardly, into different-sized pieces. Once the

cakes are completely cool, use a palette knife to spread the frosting between the layers as you stack them up. With the chocolate cut up and ready to go, ice the outside of the cake starting from the centre of the top layer, spreading the frosting out, then down and around the sides of the cake. Press the larger uniform shards around the bottom layer of the cake, and use the rest to build up around the top, then into the centre. You can use lustre dusts or edible spray paint to colour some of the chocolate if desired.

GLITTER LETTER CAKE

Choose a cake you want to make – I used the bitter chocolate orange cake recipe on page 46. Make up a batch of frosting of your choice | I used the chocolate ganache on page 259 |. To make your glitter letters you will need: a pack of gumpaste/sugarpaste in any colour, a rolling pin and a sharp knife or scalpel, a dish of water, some edible glitter and some baking paper. Here's how you do it: roll out your gumpaste to about 1–2mm thick, taking care it doesn't stick. Ideally use a silicone mat – it will make life a lot easier, although you can also use icing sugar to dust your surface and rolling pin. Use the scalpel to cut out the letters you want. Set them aside somewhere cool to set rock solid. Gently use a fingertip to brush a little water over one side of the dried letters | one at a time |, then hold over a piece of baking paper and sprinkle all over with the glitter. Tip the glitter from the baking paper back into the pot and repeat with the other letters until they are covered. Leave to dry. When your cakes have completely cooled, ice all over the cake before arranging your glitter letters on top.

LUSTRE FRUIT CAKE

Choose a cake you want to make – I used the pear and parsnip cake recipe on page 70. Make up a batch of frosting of your choice | I used the vanilla buttercream on page 254 |. When the cakes are completely cool, use a palette knife to spread frosting in between the layers and all around the outside, starting from the centre and working your way out, then down and around the sides of the cake. Dip a handful of raspberries or blackberries in lustre dust before arranging them around the cake.

SHATTERED GLASS CAKE

Choose a cake you want to make – I used the simple decadent chocolate cake recipe on page 69. Make up a batch of frosting of your choice | I used the vanilla buttercream on page 254 |. Make up a batch of sugar glass in any colour you like | see page 225 |. Leave to cool, then crack to form shards. When the cakes have cooled completely, use a palette knife to spread the frosting between the layers as you stack them up. Then ice the outside, starting from the centre of the top, spreading the icing out, then down and around the sides of the cake. Press shards of the sugar glass all over the cake so they are jutting out.

STAINED GLASS CAKE

Choose a cake you want to make – I used the margarita drizzle cake recipe | without the drizzle | on page 65. Make up a batch of frosting of your choice | I used the vanilla buttercream on page 254 |. Make up batches of sugar glass in different colours | see page 225 |. Leave them to cool, then crack them to form shards. When the cakes are completely cool, use a palette knife to spread the frosting between the layers as you stack them up. Ice the outside, starting from the centre of the top and spreading the icing out, then down and around the sides of the cake. While the frosting is still wet, gently press the shards of sugar glass all over the cake, making up any pattern you like. If your icing sets before you have a chance to attach the sugar shards, just pipe or dab a little bit of fresh frosting onto the cake and attach the glass that way.

TIP: When building a bigger cake don't use too much frosting between each layer, as the added pressure of the extra layers will force it out of the sides and spoil your decoration.

PASTRY

PASTRY

PASTRY is an unleavened dough made from flour, fat and liquid and baked to form the base for tarts, pies and sweets. There are many different types of pastry, the most familiar being shortcrust, puff, flaky (rough puff), filo and choux. Pastry-making in its various forms has a long history, spanning the globe from the ancient Mediterranean, via the Crusaders, to Italy and France and the rest of Europe.

When it comes to making pastry, confidence is key. You are sure to make a few mistakes on the path to perfection, but keep at it and practice will make perfect sooner than you think.

SHORTCRUST PASTRY

Shortcrust pastry can be used to make both sweet and savoury dishes – if you practise and gain some confidence with this basic dough, you will be set for all the rest. Standard shortcrust pastry is made with half the amount of fat to flour, and just enough cold water to bring it together. With only these three basic ingredients to work with, the quality of your pastry will depend on the ingredients you use and your technique – so don't be cheap and don't cut corners. Here's a breakdown of the ingredients:

A NOTE ON TART TINS

Use non-stick tins wherever possible when baking tarts. If you are using an unlined tin, you will have to grease the base and sides well with butter.

FLOUR: Use a soft plain flour (never a strong or bread flour) to minimise gluten development and keep the pastry 'short' and tender (less protein content in the flour means less gluten), and make sure it's as fresh as possible.

FAT: We generally use butter for pastry in the bakery, though you can use a combination of shortening (which is a solid saturated 100% fat) and butter if you prefer – shortening yields a more tender, flakier texture, but good butter wins out by a mile on flavour. Fat prevents water from hydrating the flour proteins that form gluten, keeping the gluten strands shorter (hence the term 'short'). The temperature of the fat plays an important role here: too warm and it will melt and your pastry will be claggy or break apart in the rolling, while very cold chunks will mean you have to overwork it to rub it into the flour and might suffer the same problems. A good technique is to refrigerate your butter, then grate it or cut it into small cubes and return it to the fridge before using.

LIQUID: Make sure it is chilled and that you use only as much as is necessary to bring the ingredients together into a dough. If you add too much liquid you'll be left with a sticky mess or a tough dough, but add too little and the baked pastry will fall apart.

MAKING THE DOUGH

The first stage of making shortcrust pastry calls for flour to be coated in a solid fat (e.g. butter) that has been cut into small chunks. This step gives the pastry tenderness, flakiness and 'shortness'. When the fat-coated clumps of flour are rolled out into a sheet they will form layers, and as the pastry bakes these layers melt away, leaving gaps in the structure and resulting in a texture that comes apart in 'flakes'. The coating of fat also prevents liquids from getting to the proteins in the flour and inhibits the development of gluten, which would lead to shrinkage and toughness in the finished bake. For this same reason pastry requires minimum handling – friction and body heat aid gluten development, so the less you work the dough the better.

You want the butter to remain as cold as possible to stop it melting or softening too much. A cold room helps, as does a chilled work surface (a stainless steel tray that's been in the fridge will do). Using a food processor or a mixer with the paddle attachment to make your pastry will eliminate the problem of your body temperature interfering. But if you are using your hands, run them under a cold tap and dry them completely before handling the pastry as little as possible – light hands are cool hands.

When it comes to bringing the flour and butter together to make the crumbs (this is called the breadcrumbs stage), I find the best method is to scoop up the flour and butter and brush it lightly with your thumbs across your four fingers, letting it fall back into the bowl or onto the surface. Work quickly and rotate the mixture so you are not handling the same area for too long at a time. Once you have added the liquid, you can use a cold knife to bring the pastry together.

RESTING

Once it has come together, you'll need to let the dough 'rest' to allow time for any gluten developed in the dough to relax. If you start to roll it out as soon as you have brought it together, it will still be elastic and will shrink back. Wrap the dough in clingfilm and place in the refrigerator for a minimum of an hour, or longer if possible – in the bakery we give our pastry at least 24 hours' resting time ahead of rolling out and baking.

BREADCRUMBS STAGE

BRINGING SWEET DOUGH TOGETHER

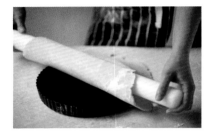

ROLLING THE PASTRY

When you remove the pastry from the refrigerator, let it sit for a while to bring it back up to room temperature before rolling – it will soften and become more manageable. Make sure that the surface on which you are going to roll out the pastry dough is clean and dry. Lightly dust the surface and your rolling pin with flour. Use light strokes and apply pressure evenly to roll out the dough – again, you don't want to overwork it. Give the dough a quarter turn periodically and flip it over from time to time, making sure you keep a floured surface at all times to prevent it from sticking. Use your rolling pin to measure your pastry against the size of your tin, then roll it out approximately 4cm wider than your tin all the way around. To transfer it to the tin, roll the pastry over the rolling pin, then unroll it into the tin and press gently into place. If baking a large tart, prick all over the base with a fork (this will release trapped air and make for a crisper base) and trim away the edges. The act of rolling will have reactivated the gluten in the flour, so you now need to put the pastry back into the fridge, in the tin, for a further hour to avoid shrinkage in the oven.

TIP: If time is short, you can leave the pastry draping over the sides of the tin, hope it doesn't crack in the oven, then trim away the excess pastry once it's baked.

A NOTE ON PASTRY WEIGHTS

Make a pastry weight you can re-use by lining your tart with a piece of clingfilm, filling with beans and twisting to seal. The clingfilm will harden in the oven and leave you with a handy little weight pouch that can be re-used.

BLIND BAKING

If you are going to fill the pastry with anything liquid you need to 'blind bake' it first so it stays firm and doesn't go soggy. To do this, you will need to weigh down the pastry so it holds its shape in the oven – line the base with baking paper or tin foil, and fill with either ceramic baking beans or any dried beans (such as black-eye or kidney beans). Once you have baked blind with the pastry weighed down, remove whatever weights and lining you have used, prick the base of the pastry and return it to the oven until it is crisp and browning. Then you can brush the pastry with egg wash | if using – see right | and put it back into the oven briefly, just to seal it. You'll know it's done when you have achieved a nice, even, light browning and the base is crisp.

EGG WASH

Using an egg wash is an optional stage, but in the bakery we always brush our pastry cases with an egg wash to seal them. We make ours with 25ml of double cream or milk for every egg yolk, whisked lightly together.

THE OVEN

Always put pastry into a preheated hot oven – if the oven is too cool the pastry will melt rather than cook. For an even, crisp base for your tart or pie, place a heavy baking sheet in the oven as it heats and place the pie dish directly onto the heated tray when ready to bake. Opening the oven door will not affect the baking of pastry as negatively as it does a cake. While it's not ideal to keep swinging the door open and letting cold air in (you want the oven to stay hot) don't be afraid to check on your pastry as it bakes.

REMEMBER

- Do not over-mix, as this produces gluten and makes the dough tougher.

- Try to work quickly, minimising the amount you're handling the pastry.

- Work in a cool room on a cold surface with cold hands. You don't want the butter to melt in the dough.

- Be precise with the measurements – use a digital scale if possible.

- Allow the dough to rest in the fridge overnight if you can.

SAVOURY SHORTCRUST PASTRY

*Add a little bit of icing sugar to this recipe to caramelise and give the pastry
a beautiful brown colour.*

225g plain flour

Pinch of salt

20g icing sugar, sifted | optional |

115g unsalted butter, cubed or grated
and refrigerated

3–4 tbsp ice cold water

One 23cm round tart tin, or one
12-hole cupcake/muffin tray

BY HAND:

1   Sift the flour, salt and icing sugar, if using, from a height onto a cool, clean, dry surface. Add the butter and work into the flour – work towards the middle, rubbing the mixture between your thumb and fingers but handling as little as possible – until it resembles rough breadcrumbs.

2   Add the water very gradually and evenly, 1 teaspoon at a time, until there's just enough to bring the dough together into one piece. Form into a round ball. Wrap in clingfilm and refrigerate for at least 30 minutes.

3   Remove the dough from the fridge, allow it to come to room temperature, and knead very gently on a lightly floured clean surface. Roll out to your desired thickness.

IN A FOOD PROCESSOR OR STAND MIXER:

1   Chill the mixing bowl and correct pastry attachment in the fridge for 30 minutes.

2   Sift the flour, salt and icing sugar, if using, into a large bowl. Add the butter, then cover with a plate and transfer to the freezer for 10 minutes.

3   Transfer to your food processor or stand mixer and combine in quick pulses to just bring it to the breadcrumbs stage.

4   Add the water gradually until it comes together as a dough.

TIP: If you are not going to use the pastry immediately, it can be wrapped and stored in the fridge for up to 3 days.

SWEET SHORTCRUST PASTRY

This is the pastry recipe we use for most of the sweet tarts we make in the bakery. Don't be afraid to experiment here — you may want to adapt the amount of sugar, butter, eggs and milk to suit your tastes. We use egg yolk to make up some of the liquid in our sweet pastry, as it enriches the flavour and texture. As always, be careful when adding liquid to your pastry as this can make or break it — add gradually, and stop when it's just enough to bring it together.

250g plain flour

100g icing sugar

Pinch of salt

150g unsalted butter, cubed or grated and refrigerated

2 egg yolks

1 egg

Optional flavourings: zest of 1 orange, lemon or grapefruit, finely grated, or 1 tsp freshly grated nutmeg, or 15g ground almonds

One 23cm round tart tin, or one 12-hole cupcake/muffin tray

BY HAND:

1 Sift the flour, icing sugar and salt from a height onto a cool, clean, dry surface. Add the butter and work into the flour — work towards the middle, rubbing the mixture between your thumb and fingers but handling it as little as possible — until it resembles rough breadcrumbs.

2 Whisk together the egg and yolks and add them to the mix — with your flavouring, if using — and use a cold knife to bring it together into a ball of dough, taking care not to over-mix. Flour lightly, pat into a flat round and wrap in clingfilm.

3 Refrigerate overnight if possible, or for a minimum of an hour. Take the dough out of the fridge an hour before you need to roll it.

IN A FOOD PROCESSOR OR STAND MIXER:

1 Chill the mixing bowl and correct pastry attachment in the fridge for 30 minutes.

2 Sift the flour, icing sugar and salt into a large bowl, add the butter, then cover with a plate and transfer to the freezer for 10 minutes.

3 Transfer to your food processor or stand mixer and combine in quick pulses to just bring it to the breadcrumbs stage.

4 Combine the eggs and your flavouring if using and add gradually to the mixture until it comes together as a dough.

5 Refrigerate overnight if possible, or for a minimum of an hour. Take the dough out of the fridge an hour before you need to roll it.

SUMMER BAKEWELLS

The true Bakewell tart has a rich history and is a fiercely guarded British tradition. The invention of the original 'Bakewell pudding' was the result of an accident. Sometime around 1860 a tart was ordered at a local inn (then named the White Horse) in the town of Bakewell. The mistress of the inn left her cook instructions on how it was to be made, but the cook misunderstood, and instead of stirring the egg mixture into the pastry, she spread it on top of the jam and baked it that way. Our Bakewells have taken on a life of their own and reign over all our other pastries in the bakery — Vogue called them 'the best in town', and we don't like to argue. We make them seasonal with fresh fruit and coulis that varies throughout the year, and with a tiny dab of almond buttercream rather than the rich fondant favoured by Mr Kipling.

PREP TIME

45 minutes

COOKING TIME

1 hour

MAKES: 12

1 batch of Sweet or Savoury Shortcrust
    Pastry | see pages 100–101 |

Egg wash: 1 egg yolk lightly beaten with
    25ml double cream or milk

1 batch of Mixed Berry Coulis
    | see page 256 |

½ batch of Frangipane | see page 258 |

20g flaked almonds, untoasted

½ batch of Almond Buttercream
    | see page 255 |

Handful of whole fresh cherries

30g flaked almonds, toasted | see page
    257 |

One 12-hole cupcake/muffin tray

1   Preheat the oven to 180°C fan assisted/gas mark 6.

2   Roll out the pastry to about 3mm thickness and cut rounds to fit your prepared cupcake/muffin tray, allowing extra to cover the sides — approximately 10cm rounds for a standard cupcake tray. Press these carefully into the cavities and refrigerate for around 30 minutes. Line, weigh down with baking beans and blind bake | see page 98 | for around 10–15 minutes, or until starting to brown. Remove from the oven, brush all over with the egg wash and bake for another 2 minutes to seal. Remove from the oven and allow to cool.

3   Spoon 2 teaspoons of the coulis into the cooled pastry cases, pipe or spoon frangipane on top to fill, then sprinkle with the untoasted flaked almonds and return to the oven to bake for 20–25 minutes, or until the frangipane is golden brown. Try to avoid opening the oven before 15 minutes have passed, as the delicate structure of the frangipane means they have a tendency to sink. Remove from the oven and place on a wire rack to cool completely.

4   Pipe each tart with a dab of almond buttercream, then top with a fresh cherry and some toasted flaked almonds.

RHUBARB BAKEWELL TARTS

As cherries have only a short season each year, we adapt our Bakewells all year round – we make so many fruit and nut combinations that we have no right calling them Bakewells at all.

PREP TIME

45 minutes

COOKING TIME

40 minutes

MAKES: 12

1 batch of Sweet or Savoury Shortcrust
   Pastry | see pages 100–101 |
Egg wash: 1 egg yolk lightly beaten with
   25ml double cream or milk
½ batch of Frangipane | see page 258 |
20g flaked almonds
2 tbsp apricot jam | optional |
1 batch of Almond or Vanilla
   Buttercream | see pages 254–255 |

FOR THE RHUBARB FILLING

300g rhubarb, trimmed and cut into
   3cm pieces
Juice and zest of 1 lemon, finely grated
80g caster sugar

FOR THE RHUBARB TOPPING

1 stem of rhubarb, trimmed and cut
   into 3cm pieces
20g caster sugar

One 12-hole cupcake/muffin tray
One baking tray, lined

VARIATION: You could make this as a big tart too. Just roll the pastry to 5mm thickness instead of 3mm and increase the baking time for the frangipane slightly.

1   Preheat the oven to 150°C fan assisted/gas mark 3.

2   Make the rhubarb filling. Place the rhubarb in a wide heavy-bottomed pan with the lemon juice and zest and add water until just covered. Add the sugar and heat to dissolve, then bring to the boil. Lower the heat and simmer for 4–5 minutes, then leave to stand for 10 minutes. Drain well, reserving the liquid. Return the liquid to the pan and boil until it's thick and syrupy – approximately 8 minutes. Add the rhubarb and turn so it's coated in the syrup glaze.

3   Make the rhubarb topping. Place the rhubarb on your prepared baking tray and sprinkle with the caster sugar. Cover with tin foil and bake for 15 minutes, checking often, until the rhubarb is just softening but still holds its shape.

4   Turn the oven up to 180°C fan assisted/gas mark 6.

5   Roll out the pastry to about 3mm thickness and cut rounds to fit your prepared cupcake/muffin tray, allowing extra to cover the sides – approximately 10cm rounds for a standard cupcake tray. Press these carefully into the cavities and refrigerate for around 30 minutes. Line, weigh down with baking beans and blind bake | see page 98 | for around 15 minutes, or until starting to brown. Remove from the oven, brush all over with the egg wash and bake for another 2 minutes to seal. Remove from the oven and cool.

6   Spoon some of the cooled rhubarb filling | not the juice | into each pastry case, followed by the frangipane | fill to just below the top |. Top with the flaked almonds and return to the oven for 20–25 minutes, or until a cocktail stick inserted into the frangipane comes out clean.

7   To make the optional glaze, mix the apricot jam with a few drops of water in a heavy-bottomed pan and heat over a medium heat until runny but not bubbling hot. Brush a little of the glaze over each tart as they come out of the oven, then allow to cool in the tins for 20 minutes. Remove and transfer to a wire rack to cool completely.

8   Top each tart with a dab of buttercream and a piece of the rhubarb.

QUINCE TART WITH STAR ANISE AND WHOLEGRAIN SPELT PASTRY

Quinces are one of my favourite fruits, lumpy and hard, awkward to work with, covered with fuzz and totally inedible when raw. But when cooked they soften up, turn a rosy hue and smell and taste like tropical, floral pears. They can be just as delicious served simply in their own syrup as in a tart: try them warm, with ice cream or natural yoghurt. They will keep in their juice for up to a week in the fridge.

PREP TIME

50 minutes, plus chilling time

COOKING TIME

1 ½ hours

SERVES: 8

1 litre water

4 large quinces | about 300g each | peeled, cored and quartered

1 lemon, sliced

1 orange, sliced

220g light brown sugar

½ vanilla pod, split lengthways

5 or 6 star anise

1 cinnamon stick

1 batch of Sweet or Savoury Shortcrust Pastry, using wholegrain spelt flour instead of plain | see pages 100–101 |

FOR THE GLAZE

Juice and finely grated zest of 1 lemon

½ tbsp clear honey

500ml of the poaching syrup plus the star anise

One 23cm round tart tin, 3–3.5cm deep

1 Put the water into a heavy-bottomed pan and set it on the stove. Add the quinces, lemon and orange slices, sugar and spices and turn the heat to medium. Stir to dissolve the sugar, then cover and leave to simmer in the syrup, stirring occasionally, until the quinces are cooked through but still firm | you can test for doneness with a fork | — depending on their ripeness and how thick the slices are they may take anything from 40 minutes to 1 hour. Make sure you check on them from time to time. When they are done, drain and reserve the poaching liquid.

2 Preheat the oven to 180°C fan assisted/gas mark 6.

3 Make the glaze. Put the lemon zest and juice, the honey, the strained poaching liquid and star anise into a separate pan and reduce over a high heat for 10–15 minutes, until slightly thickened and starting to brown. Remove from the heat and set aside.

4 Roll out the pastry to 5mm thick, place in your prepared tart tin and refrigerate for around 30 minutes. Line, weigh down with baking beans and blind bake | see page 98 | on a baking tray for 15 minutes. Remove the beans, prick the base with a fork and bake for a further 10 minutes, or until browning and starting to crisp. Brush the pastry with a thin layer of the glaze and return to the oven for 2 minutes. Remove and allow to cool.

5 Drain the cooled quince quarters, slice each one into four, and assemble the slices however you like in the baked tart case. Pour the remaining glaze over the top, and return to the oven for 15 minutes. Remove and place on a wire rack to cool completely.

TIPS ON SELECTING QUINCES: Choose quinces that are firm, with a pale yellow skin. Don't be put off if they are mottled with brown spots, as this won't affect their flavour or quality, and don't worry about the fuzz, as it can be easily washed away under the tap with your hands. Quinces that are shrivelled, soft, or brown all over are no longer fresh. Handle them carefully.

VARIATION: QUINCE FRANGIPANE TART

Use any pastry you like, blind bake | see page 98 | and cool. Make up half a batch of frangipane, using the recipe on page 258, and spread it evenly in the tart case so it comes just below the edge of the shell. Drain and slice your cooled poached quinces and press them into the frangipane – two quinces should be enough here. Bake the tart for a further 20–25 minutes in a preheated 180°C fan assisted/gas mark 6 oven, or until the frangipane is cooked through. You can cover the sides of the tart pastry with tin foil if they are looking too brown, to prevent them from burning.

OF CAKE

CHERRY, MOUNTAIN PEACH AND ALMOND TART

I love mountain peaches (sometimes called flat or doughnut peaches) — it's something about their diminutive size, funny shape and enormous and unexpected aromatic sweetness. When they are in season I make this tart every week to sell in the bakery. At another time of year you can easily substitute two regular peaches.

PREP TIME

35 minutes, plus chilling time

COOKING TIME

1 hour

SERVES: 8

1 batch of Sweet or Savoury Shortcrust
   Pastry | see pages 100–101 |
Egg wash: 1 egg yolk lightly beaten with
   25ml double cream or milk
½ batch of Frangipane | see page 258 |
4 or 5 ripe but not too soft mountain
   peaches, pitted and cut into 8 slices
100g cherries, pitted but with stems
   left on | optional |
Handful of flaked almonds
2 tbsp apricot jam | optional |

One 23cm round tart tin

1   Preheat the oven to 180°C fan assisted/gas mark 6.

2   Roll out the pastry to 5mm thick, place in your prepared tart tin and refrigerate for around 30 minutes. Line, weigh down with baking beans and blind bake | see page 98 | on a baking tray for 15 minutes. Remove the beans, prick the base with a fork and bake for a further 10 minutes, or until browning and starting to crisp. Remove from the oven, brush all over with a thin layer of egg wash and return to the oven for 2 minutes to seal. Remove and place on a wire rack to cool completely.

3   Spoon in the frangipane almost to the top and level to the edges. Press in the peaches all around the tart. Scatter with the cherries, pressed into the frangipane and with their stalks sticking out the top, and sprinkle with the flaked almonds.

4   Bake for 30–35 minutes, or until the frangipane is baked through and a skewer inserted comes out clean.

5   To make the optional glaze, mix the apricot jam with a few drops of water in a heavy-bottomed pan and heat over a medium heat until runny but not bubbling hot. Brush the glaze over the tart as it comes out of the oven. Transfer to a wire rack to cool.

HOT TODDY TARTS

The perfect tarts for a winter's day. Some time in October last year I took my first day off from the bakery with a cold, and when I was better we commemorated the occasion with 'cold week' — everything we made was inspired by things you eat when you're unwell. We made chilli and ginger brownies, honey and lemon pie, and these hot toddy tarts. We even made a batch of Berocca tea cakes on the Sunday (more or less as a joke) and in an odd turn of events Chris Moyles came in towards the end of the day and bought the lot. The chocolate pastry here deviates from standard recipes — it's more like a biscuit base and is very quick to make: no resting, kneading or rolling. I learned this method from Martin, a brilliant baker I met on the 242 night bus one summer.

PREP TIME
40 minutes, plus cooling and chilling time

COOKING TIME
25 minutes

MAKES: 12

130g unsalted butter
130g caster sugar
150g plain flour, sifted
50g cocoa powder, sifted
Pinch of sea salt | optional |
Drop of vanilla extract | optional |
1 batch of Caramelised Lemon Slices
  | see page 229 |

FOR THE FILLING
125ml double cream
200g dark chocolate
  | minimum 70% cocoa solids |
  broken into small pieces
50g burnt butter | melt the butter in
  a small heavy-bottomed pan for 2
  minutes, or until a dark tan colour,
  then remove from the heat and
  cool completely |
75ml Laphroaig, or any other whisky
  you like
Pinch of sea salt

One 12-hole cupcake/muffin tray

1 Cream together the butter and sugar until evenly mixed — approximately 1 minute. Add the flour, cocoa powder, salt and vanilla if using. Beat until everything just comes together in a big crumbly mess.

2 Press the crumbs tightly onto the base and up the sides of your prepared cupcake/muffin tray and refrigerate for 30 minutes. Line, weigh down with baking beans and blind bake | see page 98 | for 15 minutes. Remove the beans and use the back of a teaspoon to smooth out the pastry. Return to the oven for another 10 minutes, or until crisp. Remove and place on a wire rack to cool completely.

3 Preheat the oven to 180°C fan assisted/gas mark 6.

4 To make the filling, heat the cream in a heavy-bottomed pan until it's starting to simmer and light steam is coming off it. Remove from the heat and add the chocolate, leave to melt for 1 minute, then stir until fully melted and combined. Whisk in the burnt butter, whisky and salt until evenly incorporated. Allow to cool, then pour into the baked and cooled tart cases.

5 Dot all over with the caramelised lemon slices and put into the fridge for 20 minutes to set. Serve right away, or leave them in the fridge and bring to room temperature for 45 minutes before serving.

SEVEN WAYS
WITH
SWEET PASTRY

GANACHE TART WITH HONEYCOMB

FRUIT TART WITH PASSIONFRUIT
AND MINT

HOT TODDY TART

SPICED APPLE CUSTARD TART

CUSTARD TART WITH
CARAMELISED ORANGES

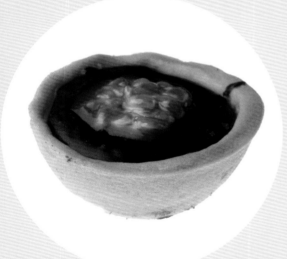

PASSIONFRUIT GANACHE TART

RHUBARB BAKEWELL TART

BANOFFEE PIE

Due to Chinese whispers (and sloppy research) I always thought banoffee pie had been invented by hungry monks and was an age-old traditional English dish. A recent fact check reveals that it was actually invented at a restaurant called the Hungry Monk in Sussex in the 1970s – oops. Feel free to add your own spices and flavourings here, use any nuts in place of the pecans, and the coffee is optional too.

PREP TIME

35 minutes, plus chilling time

COOKING TIME

35 minutes

SERVES: 8

1 batch of Sweet or Savoury Shortcrust
    Pastry | see pages 100–101 | with
    1 tsp lemon zest and 1 tsp freshly
    grated nutmeg added in the final
    stage

Egg wash: 1 egg yolk lightly beaten with
    25ml double cream or milk

400ml double cream

1 tbsp espresso powder

½ tsp vanilla extract

1 jar of dulce de leche
    | or 1 tin of Nestlé Carnation Caramel |

6 bananas, peeled and chopped

1 batch of Blanched Pecans
    | see page 216 |

¼ tsp ground cinnamon

One 23cm round tart tin

1 Preheat the oven to 180°C fan assisted/gas mark 6.

2 Roll out the pastry to 5mm thick, then place in your prepared tart tin and refrigerate for around 30 minutes. Line, weigh down with baking beans and blind bake | see page 98 | on a baking tray for 15–20 minutes. Remove the beans, prick the base with a fork and bake for a further 10 minutes, or until browning and starting to crisp. Remove from the oven, brush all over with a thin layer of egg wash, and bake for a further 2 minutes to seal. Remove and place on a wire rack to cool completely.

3 Whip up the double cream with the espresso powder and vanilla. Spread the dulce de leche in the cooled tart case, followed by the chopped bananas, the whipped cream and the cooled pecans. Sprinkle with the ground cinnamon and serve immediately.

NOTE: If you don't want to serve the pie right away, leave it until the last minute to whip the cream and assemble.

PASSIONFRUIT GANACHE TARTS

I love passionfruit. At some point or other, I've tried them in almost everything – from cakes and pies to drinks, ice creams and chocolate. I scoop them on to cakes as a garnish (just before serving) as their tartness offsets the sweetness of the cake and they lend a beautiful exotic fruitiness. These tarts are very simple but delicious. They will keep in the fridge for 3–4 days.

PREP TIME

45 minutes, plus chilling time

COOKING TIME

30 minutes

MAKES: 12

1 batch of Sweet or Savoury Shortcrust
  Pastry | see pages 100–101 |
Egg wash: 1 egg yolk lightly beaten with
  25ml double cream or milk

FOR THE PASSIONFRUIT GANACHE

200ml double cream
350g milk chocolate, broken into pieces
Flesh of 3 passionfruit, plus extra for
  topping

One 12-hole cupcake/muffin tray

1 Preheat the oven to 180°C fan assisted/gas mark 6.

2 Roll out the pastry to about 3mm thickness and cut rounds to fit your prepared cupcake/muffin tray, allowing extra to cover the sides – approximately 10cm rounds for a standard cupcake tray. Press these carefully into the cavities and refrigerate for around 30 minutes. Line, weigh down with baking beans and blind bake | see page 98 | for around 10–15 minutes, or until starting to brown. Remove from the oven, brush all over with the egg wash and bake for another 2 minutes to seal. Remove from the oven and allow to cool.

3 Make the ganache following the method on page 259 and stirring in the passionfruit flesh in the last stage. Spoon the ganache evenly into the cooled pastry cases while it's cool but still liquid | use the 'lip test' – see page 197 |. Place in the fridge to set – approximately 1 hour. Spoon the remaining passionfruit flesh on top before serving.

CUSTARD TARTS WITH CARAMELISED ORANGES

You can make these with or without the caramelised oranges; they are just as lovely with toasted nuts, or roasted rhubarb | see page 105 |.

PREP TIME

50 minutes, plus cooling time

COOKING TIME

25 minutes

MAKES: 12

1 batch of Sweet or Savoury Shortcrust
 Pastry | see pages 100–101 |

Egg wash: 1 egg yolk lightly beaten with
 25ml double cream or milk

1 batch of Simple Thick Custard,
 cooled | see page 261 |

½ batch of Oaty Crumble, cooled
 | optional – see page 128 |

1 batch of Caramelised Orange
 | or Blood Orange | Slices
 | see page 229 |

One 12-hole cupcake/muffin tray

1 Preheat the oven to 180°C fan assisted/gas mark 6.

2 Roll out the pastry to about 3mm thickness and cut rounds to fit your prepared cupcake/muffin tray, allowing extra to cover the sides – approximately 10cm rounds for a standard cupcake tray. Press these carefully into the cavities and refrigerate for around 30 minutes. Line, weigh down with baking beans and blind bake | see page 98 | for around 10–15 minutes, or until starting to brown. Remove from the oven, brush all over with the egg wash and bake for another 2 minutes to seal. Remove and allow to cool.

3 Spoon the custard evenly into the pastry cases, dust with the crumble, if using, and top each tart with an orange segment.

RHUBARB TARTS WITH CHILLI AND GINGER

Rhubarb has been used in tarts and pies for hundreds of years, so much so that it was sometimes called 'pie plant'. It's best in spring and early summer, when the fruit is juicy and the stems are hard and crisp. There are lots of beautiful flavours in the stewed rhubarb here, and it's delicious served just on its own with ice cream | see page 241 |, with natural yoghurt, or with custard | see page 260 | and crumble | see page 128 |. We've even made it into a jelly, with great results | see variation below |.

PREP TIME

3 hour and **15** minutes, plus chilling time

COOKING TIME

45 minutes

MAKES: 12

350ml water

175g caster sugar

125g root ginger, peeled and roughly chopped

1 small fresh red chilli, deseeded and roughly chopped

1 chamomile tea bag

4 large stems of rhubarb

| approximately 400g | washed, trimmed and chopped into 1cm pieces

1 batch of Sweet or Savoury Shortcrust Pastry | see pages 100–101 |

Egg wash: 1 egg yolk lightly beaten with 25ml double cream or milk

1 batch of Simple Thick Custard | see page 261 |, cooled

½ batch of Oaty Crumble | see page 128 |, cooled

One 12-hole cupcake/muffin tray

1 Preheat the oven to 180°C fan assisted/gas mark 6.

2 Make a light syrup by heating the water, caster sugar, ginger, chilli and chamomile tea bag in a heavy-bottomed pan over a medium heat, stirring occasionally until all the sugar dissolves. Bring to the boil for 2 minutes, then turn off the heat and leave to cool.

3 Remove the ginger, chilli and tea bag. Strain the syrup back into the pan, add the rhubarb and heat for 10 minutes over a medium heat. Leave to cool completely in the syrup.

4 Roll out the pastry to about 3mm thickness and cut rounds to fit your prepared cupcake/muffin tray, allowing extra to cover the sides – approximately 10cm rounds for a standard cupcake tray. Press these carefully into the cavities and refrigerate for around 30 minutes. Line, weigh down with baking beans and blind bake | see page 98 | for around 10–15 minutes, or until starting to brown. Remove, brush all over with the egg wash and bake for another 2 minutes to seal. Remove from the oven and allow to cool.

5 Spoon the cooled rhubarb evenly into the pastry cases, top with the cooled custard, then with the crumble, and serve.

VARIATION: Strain off the excess syrup from the rhubarb and add 4 tablespoons of agar flakes to make a delicious jelly. Follow the instructions on the agar pack as to method.

FRUIT TARTS WITH PASSIONFRUIT AND MINT

I originally made these fruit tarts for an Edwardian-themed event, and then made them again for a pop-up tea room in a Victorian townhouse in Dalston. They are simple to make but so pretty – perfect for a tea party or as a canapé with cocktails. If you prefer, omit the custard and serve the fruit mix directly in the crisp cooled tart cases.

PREP TIME

50 minutes, plus chilling time

COOKING TIME

25 minutes

MAKES: 12

1 batch of Sweet or Savoury Shortcrust
   Pastry | see pages 100–101 |

Egg wash: 1 egg yolk lightly beaten with
   25ml double cream or milk

300g fresh berries or other fruit,
   chopped – raspberries, strawberries,
   blueberries and peaches work well

Flesh of 4 passionfruit

1½ tbsp finely chopped fresh mint
   leaves

1 batch of Simple Thick Custard,
   cooled | see page 261 |

One 12-hole cupcake/muffin tray

1   Preheat the oven to 180°C fan assisted/gas mark 6.

2   Roll out the pastry to about 3mm thickness and cut rounds to fit your prepared cupcake/muffin tray, allowing extra to come up a little at the sides – approximately 10cm rounds for a standard cupcake tray. Press these carefully into the cavities and refrigerate for around 30 minutes. Line, weigh down with baking beans and blind bake | see page 98 | for around 10–15 minutes, or until starting to brown. Remove from the oven, brush all over with a thin layer of the egg wash and bake another 2 minutes to seal. Remove and allow to cool.

3   In a bowl, mix together the chopped fruit, passionfruit flesh and mint. Spoon the custard evenly into the pastry cases and top with the fruit.

SPICED APPLE CUSTARD TARTS

These little apple tarts are popular in the bakery in winter, and you could easily make a larger version to cut up and share. Edible blue cornflowers make a pretty decoration if you can find them – I much prefer using something natural like this to sugary sprinkles. This tart is delicious warm, with a scoop of vanilla ice cream | see page 241 |.

PREP TIME

50 minutes

COOKING TIME

25 minutes

MAKES: 12

1 batch of Sweet or Savoury Shortcrust
 Pastry | see pages 100–101 |

Egg wash: 1 egg yolk lightly beaten with
 25ml double cream or milk

25g unsalted butter

100g dark brown sugar

2 Bramley cooking apples, peeled,
 cored and sliced | place in a bowl of
 water with a dash of lemon juice to
 prevent browning |

1 star anise

¼ tsp ground cinnamon

¼ tsp freshly grated nutmeg

1 batch of Simple Thick Custard
 | see page 261 |, cooled

¼ batch of Oaty Crumble, cooled
 | see page 128 |

Handful of dried edible cornflowers or
 crystallised flowers | optional – see
 page 230 |

One 12-hole cupcake/muffin tray

1   Preheat the oven to 180°C fan assisted/gas mark 6.

2   Roll out the pastry to about 3mm thickness and cut rounds to fit your prepared cupcake/muffin tray, allowing extra to cover the sides – approximately 10cm rounds for a standard cupcake tray. Press these carefully into the cavities and refrigerate for around 30 minutes. Line, weigh down with baking beans and blind bake | see page 98 | for around 10–15 minutes, or until starting to brown. Remove from the oven, brush all over with a thin layer of the egg wash and bake for another 2 minutes to seal. Remove and allow to cool.

3   Place the butter and sugar in a pan over a medium heat. Bring to the boil, add the apples, star anise, cinnamon and nutmeg and simmer for around 5 minutes – cook until the apple is softened but still holds its shape. Remove from the heat and leave to cool and infuse with the spices.

4   Drain the apples and put 2 or 3 pieces into each pastry case. Fill with the custard, then the crumble, and decorate with edible flowers if using.

OATY CRUMBLE

Crumble is a handy recipe to learn by heart, as it's quick and easy to put together last minute, wherever you may be — you can usually scrape together the ingredients you need from anyone's larder. It will pull together any fruity or creamy dessert — dust it on top of banana and yoghurt, on ice cream | see page 241 | with some fruit or coulis | see page 256 | or on top of your trifle | see page 85 |. You can alter it to suit your palate — some people add nuts and spices, but I prefer a simple, buttery, crunchy crumble, with a pinch of sea salt for my savoury tooth. Keeps for up to two weeks if stored airtight and dry in the fridge.

PREP TIME

15 minutes, plus chilling time

COOKING TIME

15 minutes

MAKES: 400g

110g unsalted butter, cubed and
   refrigerated

110g oats

110g plain flour

110g dark brown sugar

Pinch of sea salt

One baking tray, lined

1   Preheat the oven to 180°C fan assisted/gas mark 6.

2   Put all the ingredients into a bowl and rub together with your fingers to form breadcrumbs. Spread the mixture on the lined baking tray and put into the freezer for 10 minutes | this will firm up the butter that you've softened with your hands |.

3   Transfer to the oven and bake for 10–15 minutes. Remove and allow to cool completely before crushing up with your hands or a rolling pin.

RHUBARB AND GOOSEBERRY CRUMBLE

PREP TIME

20 minutes

COOKING TIME

40 minutes

SERVES: 6

12 rhubarb stalks | approximately 600g |
400g gooseberries
Juice and finely grated zest of 1 lemon
150g light brown sugar
1 batch of Oaty Crumble
   | see page 128 |, baked and cooled

One 25 x 20cm rectangular pie dish

1   Preheat the oven to 180°C fan assisted/gas mark 6.

2   Wash all the fruit, then trim the rhubarb and cut the stems into 5–6cm chunks. Place the rhubarb and gooseberries in your pie dish and sprinkle with the lemon juice, zest and sugar. Bake for 10 minutes.

3   Remove from the oven and sprinkle all over with the crumble, making sure you don't pack it too tight. Bake for another 20–30 minutes. Remove from the oven and serve hot with ice cream | see page 241 |, double cream, custard | see page 260 | or yoghurt.

BLACKBERRY, PEAR AND PINENUT CRUMBLE

PREP TIME

20 minutes

COOKING TIME

35 minutes

SERVES: 6

8 medium ripe English pears, cored,
   peeled and sliced lengthways into
   1.5cm thick slices
100g light brown sugar
275g blackberries
60g pine nuts
1 batch of Oaty Crumble
   | see page 128 |, baked and cooled

One 30 x 20cm pie dish

1   Preheat the oven to 170°C fan assisted/gas mark 5.

2   Place the sliced pears and the sugar in a heavy-bottomed pan and cook gently over a medium heat until the fruit begins to soften and starts releasing its juice – approximately 7 minutes, depending on the ripeness. Add the blackberries and bring to the boil. Spoon into your pie dish.

3   Allow the fruit to cool just slightly, then toss the pine nuts in with your crumble and sprinkle evenly over the top of the fruit.

4   Bake for 20 minutes, or until the pine nuts are starting to turn a light golden brown. Serve hot with ice cream | see page 241 |, double cream, custard | see page 260 | or yoghurt.

BISCUITS AND TEA CAKES

BISCUITS

THIS CHAPTER covers biscuits, cookies and tea cakes. The term 'biscuit' comes from the French meaning 'twice cooked', and recalls an era when biscuits were the stuff of adventure and long voyages: hard-wearing food that lasted for ever and stored well, for when fresh food was unavailable. Modern-day biscuits vary greatly, from American drop cookies, to shortbread and biscotti, so this is just a small collection from a wide range. I have also included tea cakes in this chapter, and there is no real overarching thread, except that you could think of it as a chapter for small things you might serve with tea or coffee.

MAKE YOUR OWN BESPOKE BISCUIT CUTTERS

This is a very handy and simple technique for making your own bespoke biscuit cutters. If you can't find aluminium flashing, you can use those foil trays you get from most corner shops – look for the biggest one you can find.

String

Template of the shape you want your
  cutter to be | made out of thick card
  or a thin piece of plastic |

Ruler and pencil

Roll of aluminium flashing | you can get
  this in most hardware shops – just make
  sure it's food safe |

Good scissors

Knife

Adhesive | make sure it is non-toxic |
  or staples

1 Run the string around the edge of the template to measure the perimeter of your shape. Measure the length of the string and use a ruler to mark out a long rectangular strip the same length and approximately 6cm wide on your aluminium sheet. Now use your ruler and a knife to score down the lines before cutting out the strip with the scissors.

2 Fold over the long sharp edges of the strip so that they overlap but do not reach the opposite edge. Press down very hard along the strip using a heavy object, so that the edge is blunt but very fine.

3 Now wrap the strip around your template, bending it to set its shape. You can use any straight edges, corners or rounds on objects around the house to wrap the strip and secure its shape. Use the staples or adhesive to carefully attach the ends. Now you're ready to start cutting biscuits.

HOW TO MAKE GLITTER BISCUITS AND COOKIES

These make beautiful cake toppers or can be served on their own. You can find edible glitter at most cake supply shops, and easily online.

Make up a batch of biscuits using any recipe you like. Once cooled, dip a clean finger into a bowl of water and brush lightly over the surface of one of the biscuits, just enough to wet it but not soak it. Hold the biscuit over a sheet of foil or baking paper and tip edible glitter over it so that it coats the surface. Carefully shake any excess glitter off and tip it back into the pot. Repeat with the rest of the biscuits.

TEA CAKES AND SWEET DOUGHS

SOME of the tea cakes in this book – the Chelsea buns and brioche, for example – are made with a sweet dough. Different from cakes in lots of ways, they use yeast as a raising agent, contain strong flour for its high protein content and take longer to prepare. Working with sweet dough requires a basic understanding of bread-making, an art that's often mystified but is really quite simple. Some of the basic method is broken down here.

MAKING THE DOUGH

The basic ingredients of a sweet dough are flour, water, milk, butter, eggs, sugar, yeast and salt. The presence of liquid causes proteins in the flour to come together and form gluten. In this case we want to encourage the development of the gluten rather than limit it. Stretching and kneading the dough helps develop a gluten structure, forming an elastic 'web' that can stretch to expand and trap pockets of air. This step will also ensure that the yeast is evenly distributed within the dough.

NOTE: We use fresh yeast in the bakery as it yields a nicer flavour, but if you can't source fresh yeast you can substitute 5g of fast-action dried yeast for every 10g of fresh.

KNEADING

This is one of the most important stages of making a dough, and requires the most effort on your part. To achieve a beautiful dough you will need to work it for around 30 minutes, using any method you like – pushing, pulling, twisting, stretching – just keeping your goal in mind: you want to develop the gluten within the dough. It is helpful to think of the dough as a big piece of gum being chewed – it starts off brittle and by aggravation gets stretchier and more elastic. You also want to keep the dough's temperature up during this stage – work it too slowly and the temperature will drop.

A NOTE ON SALT

Direct contact with salt will cause yeast to expire; however, in the moderation of the dough salt will regulate the yeast's activity in a helpful way. Salt also helps to strengthen gluten, adds flavour and acts as a preservative.

THE BUBBLEGUM TEST

A NOTE ON AMYLASE

The liquid in your dough has activated amylase, an enzyme present in the flour. This enzyme breaks down starch into sugars, for the yeast to feed off while the dough is resting.

THE BUBBLEGUM TEST

To check when your dough is ready, you can test for doneness using the bubblegum test.

Take a piece of dough and stretch it lightly between your fingers, simulating the stretching that will be caused by the carbon dioxide released within the dough; when you hold it up to a light you should be able to see your fingers clearly though the other side and it will take on a transparent, parchment-like quality.

TIP: Don't flour the surface you're kneading on – the table will grip the dough as you work and you'll be stretching the gluten further and developing it more quickly. Don't be afraid of a sticky dough. Flour is absorbent, and if you have a dry dough to start off with it will just keep getting drier.

RESTING THE DOUGH

After you have kneaded the dough, you must leave it to rest. Resting the dough gives the yeast a chance to work, feeding off the sugars and releasing carbon dioxide, causing the dough to stretch and rise. If the dough has a good gluten structure within it, the released gases will be contained in 'pockets' and will help to give the dough a light texture. The conditions needed for this step are warmth and slight humidity. The warmth is easy enough – a warm room or somewhere close by the oven will do. Humidity can be achieved by wrapping the bowl with clingfilm or draping a hot, slightly damp cloth over it. Your aim is to prevent the skin of the dough from drying out and restricting its rise.

SHAPING

After leaving the dough to rest, it must be shaped to form your buns or rolls – this stage will give the dough tension, without which it will lose its shape during proving and baking. Follow the instructions given for shaping in each recipe.

PROVING

During shaping, some of the carbon dioxide will have been knocked out of the dough and it needs another opportunity to rise. The yeast will become inactive shortly after entering the oven, so this extra stage gives it a last chance to aerate the dough. To make a home prover:

1 Place the dough in a tin on a shelf in a cold oven.

2 Place a heatproof pan or glass bowl half filled with boiling water in the bottom of the oven and quickly close the door. The steam will provide the humidity needed and bring the temperature in the oven up to about 30°C.

3 After 20 minutes, take the dough out of the oven and press a finger into the surface – if it springs back and doesn't leave an indentation it's ready (this indicates that the yeast is active and producing CO2). If you press the dough and there is no springback at all, it has over-proved – the best thing you can do is get it into a hot oven as soon as possible. A sign of an under-proved dough is an uneven texture, ranging from 'open' near the crust and getting increasingly smaller towards the base.

NOTE: Do not open the oven door during this proving period. If you do, replace the boiling water immediately.

BAKING

There are different methods to test for doneness. Colour and crust will give an indication – check each individual recipe for indicators.

TEMPERATURE

Yeast is a single-cell organism that thrives in similar conditions to us humans. At cold temperatures it will become relatively inactive and metabolise at a slow rate, and any temperature over 60°C will kill it (the continued rise of a dough in the oven is caused by expanding gases – no more carbon dioxide is released). Yeast is happiest at about 27–30°C, when it feeds, multiplies, metabolises at an optimum rate and releases higher levels of carbon dioxide. Working your dough and a warm environment will keep it at its optimum temperature.

SHORTBREAD

The classic shortbread method calls for a solid fat (like butter) to be coated onto dry ingredients at the start of the recipe. As with making pastry, this step reduces gluten development and makes for a flaky, 'short' finished product. As with pastry again, shortbread requires minimal mixing. Once the dry ingredients and the wet ingredients have come together, the less you work the dough the better – excess gluten formation leads to shrinkage and toughness in the finished bake.

PREP TIME

15 minutes, plus chilling time

COOKING TIME

12 minutes

MAKES: 12 large or **30** mini shortbreads

300g white spelt flour

75g caster sugar, plus extra for dusting

25g icing sugar

Pinch of sea salt

250g unsalted butter, cubed and
  refrigerated

1 egg yolk

1 tsp vanilla extract

One large baking tray, lined

1   Sift the flour, sugars and salt together in a large bowl. Now add the cold butter and rub with your fingertips to form fine breadcrumbs. Add the egg yolk and vanilla and bring the mixture together into a dough, being careful not to overwork it.

2   Roll out on a floured surface to approximately 1cm thick. Cut into circles using an 8cm cookie cutter | or 5cm if you prefer mini shortbreads |, place on your prepared baking tray and refrigerate for a minimum of 2 hours, but preferably overnight.

3   Preheat the oven to 180°C fan assisted/gas mark 6.

4   Bake for approximately 12 minutes, or until the edges are just starting to brown. Remove from the oven, cool on the tray for a couple of minutes, then transfer to a wire rack, dust the tops with sugar and leave to cool completely.

THREE WAYS WITH SHORTBREAD

MINI LAVENDER SHORTBREAD
Perfect with fresh summer lemonade. Add a good pinch of dried lavender, ground in a pestle and mortar, when you are sifting together the flour, sugar and salt. Use a 2.5cm cutter to make these mini shortbreads.

LEMON PISTACHIO SHORTBREAD
A nutty, citrus variation. Add the finely grated zest of 1 lemon and 70g pistachios, crushed in a pestle and mortar, when you are sifting together the flour, sugar and salt.

BASIL SHORTBREAD
Rosemary works well here too, for a sweet, buttery and savoury shortbread. Add 5 basil leaves, chopped very fine, when you are sifting together the flour, sugar and salt.

CHOCOLATE CHIP COOKIES

These cookies were an obsession when I was younger – achieving the ultimate chocolate chip cookie recipe was one of the first things that drew me to baking. The perfect balance of soft, crisp, chewy, chocolatey, buttery and salty is the sort of thing that can drive a person to distraction. You may want to alter this recipe to suit your own tastes, but this is as close to perfect as it gets for me. Experiment with different salts if you come across them – they are the crowning glory of a good chocolate chip cookie.

PREP TIME

30 minutes

COOKING TIME

13 minutes | per batch |

MAKES: 28

430g plain flour, sifted

1 ½ tsp bicarbonate of soda

Pinch of salt

240g unsalted butter, room temperature

230g light brown sugar

200g caster sugar

2 eggs

⅔ tsp vanilla extract

140g very dark chocolate, roughly chopped

Sprinkling of sea salt | I use Hawaiian Black Lava Salt |

Two or three baking trays, lined

1   Preheat the oven to 180°C fan assisted/gas mark 6.

2   In a bowl, whisk together the flour, bicarbonate of soda and salt and set aside.

3   Cream the butter and sugars together for 2 minutes. Gradually add the eggs, then the vanilla. Now gently add the flour mix and fold in the chocolate.

4   When the dough has come together, break off pieces and form them into balls roughly the size of a golf ball. Press gently down onto your prepared baking trays, leaving a good 8cm between them. Sprinkle the top of each cookie with the salt.

5   Bake in batches for 8 minutes, then gently press each cookie flat with a spatula | this is optional – you may prefer to leave them to rise slightly |. Bake for another 3–5 minutes, or until lightly brown.

6   Remove from the oven and allow to cool on the trays for 10 minutes before transferring them to a wire rack to cool completely.

NOTE: You can store the dough unbaked in the fridge for up to three days, and slice off pieces to bake.

SPICY GINGERY GINGERBREAD

I love ginger and I love biscuits, but I always felt let down by gingerbread because it's often dry and dense, with not enough flavour. In the bakery, we've adapted our gingerbread over time to make it softer, spicier and more gingery – this is the recipe we were using over Christmas last year, and it goes well with absinthe hot chocolate | see page 206 for recipe |. If you can't take the heat, experiment with reducing the chilli, ginger and spices. If you have one, use a spice grinder to grind up the spices, otherwise you'll have to make do with a pestle and mortar and some elbow grease.

NOTE: Yolks in a batter in place of whole eggs will increase moisture and soften the texture.

PREP TIME
30 minutes, plus chilling time

COOKING TIME
20 minutes

MAKES: 20

I egg
I egg yolk
200g unsalted butter, room
   temperature
200g dark brown sugar
I15g golden syrup
80g root ginger, peeled and finely
   grated
½ fresh mild or medium
   | according to taste | red chilli,
   deseeded and finely chopped
12g ground ginger
5g ground cinnamon
5g freshly grated nutmeg
5g ground cloves
3g cardamom seeds, ground as finely
   as possible
3g cracked black pepper
560g plain flour, sifted
3g fine salt
¼ tsp bicarbonate of soda

Two baking trays, lined

1 In a bowl, lightly beat together the egg and the egg yolk and set aside.

2 In a second bowl, beat the butter, sugar and syrup together until very light and fluffy – approximately 6–7 minutes. Gradually add the beaten eggs, beating just to combine everything.

3 Mix together the ginger, chilli and spices and add them to the batter. Then add the flour, salt and bicarbonate of soda and beat to bring it all together into a dough. Wrap the dough in clingfilm and refrigerate for a minimum of 20 minutes.

4 Preheat the oven to 180°C fan assisted/gas mark 6.

5 Remove the dough from the fridge and allow it to come to room temperature, so it's soft enough to roll. Lightly flour a clean, dry surface and your rolling pin and roll the dough out to approximately Icm thick.

6 Cut out rounds using a 10cm biscuit cutter | or any size and shape you like – remember to adjust the baking time accordingly |. Transfer them to your prepared baking trays and bake for 15–20 minutes, or until golden brown.

7 Remove from the oven and allow to cool on the trays for 10 minutes before transferring to a wire rack to cool completely.

NOTE: Scrape down the bowl after each addition.

BROWNIE

According to some accounts, brownies were another bakery staple born of an accident — in this case it was leavening omitted from a chocolate cake. Modern recipes vary greatly, but there are a few tricks I have learned over the years for making a great batch. First, you can beat the eggs and sugar on a high speed to make a semi-meringue, which gives the top that amazing shine. Another is to use both cocoa and chocolate, and a third is to include a bit of self-raising flour — this gives the mixture just a tiny bit of leavening, but as the batter is so dense and heavy it will drop back down, giving it an extra rich, fudgy texture as in this recipe here. Brownies are delicious eaten warm with vanilla ice cream | see page 241 | or about 30 minutes after removing them from the fridge. They will keep wrapped airtight for a week.

PREP TIME

25 minutes

COOKING TIME

18 minutes

MAKES: 12

5 medium eggs

300g dark chocolate

| minimum 70% cocoa solids |

broken into pieces

300g unsalted butter, room

temperature, cubed

400g caster sugar

80g cocoa powder, sifted

130g self-raising flour, sifted

70g plain flour, sifted

50g nuts of your choice — I like pecans,

roughly chopped walnuts

and pistachios

1 tsp vanilla extract

Sprinkling of sea salt

One 25cm square cake tin, lined

1 Preheat the oven to 180°C fan assisted/gas mark 6.

2 Whisk the eggs in a bowl, then add the chocolate and set aside.

3 Melt the butter in a pan, then add the sugar and stir until dissolved. Pour into the bowl with the chocolate and eggs, stir to melt, then beat for 3–4 minutes.

4 In another bowl, whisk together the cocoa powder and flours and fold into the chocolate mix. Stir in the nuts and vanilla.

5 Transfer to your prepared tin, sprinkle with sea salt and bake for 18 minutes, or until you have a crisp top and a middle that wobbles when you gently shake the tray. Remove from the oven and leave to cool and set in the tin before eating warm, or transfer to the fridge to eat later.

BROWNIE PYRAMID

This was invented by one of my bakers when he was a kid. We actually made one once for a customer who requested 'something very chocolatey and very extravagant'. The structure is pretty solid, so you can build it as tall as you like – just keep an even progression between the size of the tiers (so if your base tier is 25cm and the next tier up is 20cm, make the following tier 15cm and so on).

1 batch of Brownies | see page 147 |
  | or as many batches as you need to
  achieve your perfect tower |
Small amount of melted chocolate
  for attaching
1 batch of Ganache Glaze | or as much
  as you need – see page 259 |
Fresh fruit, flowers or Popping Candy
  'Fool's Gold' | see page 205 |
  to decorate

1 Use a ruler and a sharp knife to cut squares from your brownie sheet in different sizes. Use a little bit of melted chocolate to stick them together, one on top of the other, in descending size order.

2 Pour the ganache glaze carefully over your structure, using a palette knife to smooth out each layer. Then decorate however you like.

BISCUIT BROWNIES

These biscuits have the brownie qualities of a fudgy chocolate middle and a perfect crisp finish. The trick is in the timing, so make sure you keep an eye on them in the final minutes – they will start to crack only at the very end. Try adding chopped nuts, or white and milk chocolate chips.

PREP TIME

20 minutes, plus chilling time

COOKING TIME

24 minutes | in 3 batches |

MAKES: 15

160g plain flour, sifted

⅓ tsp baking powder

Pinch of sea salt

30g unsalted butter, room temperature, cubed

300g dark chocolate

| minimum 70% cocoa solids | broken into pieces

4 eggs

175g caster sugar | use vanilla caster sugar if you have it – see page 228 |

30g flaked almonds

One baking tray, lined

1   In a bowl, whisk together the flour, baking powder and salt and set aside.

2   Melt the butter and chocolate together in a double boiler | see page 196 |. Remove from the heat as soon as everything is melted and stir to bring it together. Set aside and allow to cool a little.

3   Beat the eggs and the sugar together for 2–3 minutes, until pale and slightly thickened. Fold in the chocolate mix, then stir in the flour mix. Refrigerate for a minimum of 40 minutes.

4   Preheat the oven to 180°C fan assisted/gas mark 6.

5   Remove from the fridge. Scoop up dessert spoon-sized chunks of dough, round them with your hands and press them onto the prepared baking tray, leaving a 5cm gap between them | you will most likely need to bake them in three batches |. Press almond flakes into the top of each one and bake for 10–12 minutes, or until the tops are shiny and cracked – watch carefully for the cracking stage, and as soon as the biscuits have cracked all the way across the top take them out of the oven immediately. Leave them on the tray for 5 minutes, then carefully transfer them to a wire rack to cool completely.

NANA'S SCONE

This was my boyfriend's grandma's recipe on his mother's side – she was a prolific cook and baker, as is his ma. I never met his grandma but have been lucky enough to learn some of her baking tips and recipes. This is a lovely buttery and light scone with a hint of saltiness that's perfect with lots of jam and cream. The brown sugar on top is our addition and gives the scones a lovely caramel crunch. We've tweaked the recipe over time, but we still always call them Nana's scones.

PREP TIME

20 minutes, plus chilling time

COOKING TIME

12 minutes

MAKES: 12

500g self-raising flour, sifted

30g caster sugar

Pinch of sea salt

170g unsalted butter, cubed and
    refrigerated

1 large egg

250ml whole milk

Egg wash: 1 egg yolk lightly beaten with
    25ml double cream or milk

1 tbsp light brown sugar

One baking tray, lined

1 If making by hand, whisk together the flour, sugar and salt in a bowl. Add the butter and pass it through your fingertips lightly, thumbs across fingers, to make breadcrumbs – the aim here is to coat the flour in the butter, not rub it in, so keep your fingers light and fast. This may take 5 minutes or so. Alternatively you can use a food processor for this first stage.

2 In a small jug, whisk together the egg and milk, then pour it into the bowl and mix with a spoon or fork. The mixture will be quite sticky, so lightly dust it with flour and shape it into a ball. Wrap the dough in clingfilm and refrigerate for a minimum of 20 minutes.

3 Preheat the oven to 200°C fan assisted/gas mark 8.

4 Remove the dough from the fridge and gently press it out on a lightly floured surface to a 3cm thickness. Cut out rounds using a 6cm cutter and place on your prepared baking tray, leaving a little room for expansion. Brush the tops with a thin layer of egg wash, sprinkle with brown sugar and bake for 10–12 minutes, or until just lightly browning.

5 Remove and allow to cool on the tray for 10 minutes before transferring to a wire rack to cool completely.

VARIATION: Add 40g of dried fruit soaked in stout and spices to this recipe for extra flavour. Method: Put the fruit into a bowl, cover with stout | or Guinness will do | and add a star anise and a cinnamon stick. Leave to soak for 2 days, then remove the spices and add to the dough at step 2.

HOW TO MAKE YOUR OWN BUTTER AND BUTTERMILK

Making your own butter is simple and much quicker than you would imagine, plus you get a delicious result and can use the buttermilk in lots of baking recipes – from soda bread and scones to the red velvet cake on page 72.

Buttermilk is an acidic ingredient so make sure you balance it if you are going to add it to a recipe – you will find bicarbonate of soda is used as a leavening agent in most recipes that call for buttermilk.

MAKES about **500g** butter and **500ml** buttermilk

I litre double cream, room temperature

I tsp dairy salt | optional |

Greaseproof/waxed paper

Tin foil

1 Soak the butter bats in iced water for around 30 minutes ahead of using.

2 Place the clean metal bowl of your stand mixer in the freezer or fridge. Once cool, pour the double cream into your cold, dry mixing bowl and whisk at a medium speed until thick. It will go through the thickening stages you'll recognise if you have whipped cream in the past. Continue whipping until the cream collapses and separates. You will have both liquid | buttermilk | and solid | butter | in the bowl.

3 Drain the buttermilk through a clean sieve or cheesecloth into a bowl. There will still be traces of buttermilk in your newly formed butter, so wash and dry your bowl and return the butter solids to whisk for another minute or so. Drain as before,

then transfer the butter to a clean bowl and cover with very cold water. Use butter bats or clean hands to knead the butter and force out any remaining buttermilk. | If any buttermilk is left in the butter it will sour quickly and ruin your butter, so be thorough. | Drain the butter and rinse with cold water until it runs clear.

4 Separate the butter into two bars, then use the cold, dry bats or cold hands to pat them into the shape you want. Wrap in greaseproof/waxed paper, then in foil, and store in the coldest part of the fridge, away from any strong odours. It should keep well, but if you are unsure and want to check its freshness, cut a small slice away from the edge of the butter. If the colour is different inside, it's going off.

WHOLEGRAIN SPELT SCONES

These scones have a lovely hearty depth of flavour, and a sprinkling of ground hazelnuts really brings out the nutty essence of the spelt. If you like a hint of savoury, try adding a pinch of sea salt. Either way they are delicious with jam, butter and fresh strawberries.

PREP TIME

20 minutes, plus chilling time

COOKING TIME

15 minutes

MAKES: 12

500g wholegrain spelt flour, sifted

1 tbsp baking powder

4 tbsp dark brown sugar, plus extra
    for sprinkling

2 pinches of salt | optional |

170g unsalted butter, melted

250ml whole milk

1 egg

Handful of blanched hazelnuts, ground in
    a food processor | optional |

Egg wash: 1 egg yolk lightly beaten with
    25ml double cream or milk

One baking tray, lined

1   If making by hand, put the flour, baking powder, sugar and salt, if using, into a bowl and whisk together. Add the butter and pass it through your fingertips lightly, thumbs across fingers, to make breadcrumbs – the aim here is to coat the flour in the butter, not rub it in, so keep your fingers light and fast. This may take 5 minutes or so. Alternatively you can use a food processor for this first stage.

2   Now add the milk and egg, and with well-floured hands bring the mixture together to form a dough. Lightly dust it with flour and shape it into a ball. Wrap the dough in clingfilm and refrigerate for a minimum of 20 minutes.

3   Preheat the oven to 190°C fan assisted/gas mark 7.

4   Remove the dough from the fridge and gently roll out to 3cm thickness on a lightly floured surface. Cut out rounds using a 6cm cutter and place on your prepared baking tray, leaving a little room for expansion. Brush the tops with a thin layer of egg wash, sprinkle with brown sugar and the ground hazelnuts, if using, and bake for 15 minutes, or until just lightly browning. Remove from the oven and allow to cool on the tray for 10 minutes before transferring to a wire rack to cool completely.

REDCURRANT FRIANDS

These very light cakes use egg whites for leavening, icing sugar for sweetness and ground almonds for a delicious texture that's chewy and moist. I love them with the bitterness of English currants, but try them with any tart summer berries. These are delicious eaten fresh from the oven, and they keep well for 2–3 days.

PREP TIME

25 minutes

COOKING TIME

20 minutes

MAKES: 12

90g plain flour, sifted

200g icing sugar, sifted

Good pinch of sea salt

180g ground almonds

Finely grated zest of 2 lemons

6 egg whites

200g unsalted butter, melted
completely and cooled

Handful of redcurrants or
blackcurrants, de-stemmed

20g flaked almonds

One 12-hole cupcake or muffin tray,
greased | a silicone tray is best here |

1 Preheat the oven to 180°C fan assisted/gas mark 6.

2 Whisk together the flour and icing sugar in a bowl, then whisk in the salt, ground almonds and lemon zest.

3 Whip up the egg whites until stiff peaks form | see page 35 |. Fold the whites into the dry ingredients | see page 35 |, then lightly stir in the melted butter. It should come together into a batter.

4 Spoon evenly into your prepared cupcake or muffin tray and press a few of the berries into each one. Scatter all over with the flaked almonds and bake for 15–20 minutes, or until a cocktail stick inserted into the centre comes out clean | avoid skewering the fruit, as this may result in the stick coming out clean before it's baked properly |. Allow to cool in the tin for 10 minutes before transferring onto a wire rack to cool completely.

BACON AND MAPLE SYRUP TEA CAKES

*I first made these tea cakes for a breakfast event with jelly experimenters Bompas and Parr;
the theme was 'meat', the centrepiece a hog's head. Never knowingly doing anything by halves,
or even two-thirds, they had decorated their kitchen with huge illustrations of animals divided
into their cuts of meat. They served champagne with strawberries injected with ether,
and I made these breakfast tea cakes that echo the flavours of a traditional American
French toast and bacon breakfast.*

PREP TIME

40 minutes

COOKING TIME

45 minutes

MAKES: 12

180g plain flour, sifted

½ tsp baking powder

½ tsp salt

½ freshly grated nutmeg

Pinch of ground cinnamon

170g unsalted butter, room
    temperature

215g caster sugar

3 eggs, separated

1 tsp vanilla extract

125ml whole milk

12 whole pecans, toasted | see page
    257 |

Drizzle of maple syrup, to decorate

Cracked black pepper

FOR THE CARAMELISED BACON

3 rashers of smoked back bacon

1 tbsp maple syrup, for brushing

One 12-hole cupcake/muffin tray,
    well greased

One baking tray, lined with foil

1   Preheat the oven to 180°C fan assisted/gas mark 6.

2   In a bowl, whisk together the flour, baking powder, salt and spices
    and set aside.

3   Cream the butter and sugar together until very light and fluffy –
    approximately 7–10 minutes. Add the egg yolks one at a time,
    beating until just evenly incorporated. Add the vanilla.

4   Now add the dry ingredients in three parts, alternating with the
    milk, beginning and ending with the dry, and mix evenly.

5   In a bowl, beat the egg whites until stiff peaks form | see page 35 |.
    Gently fold the whites into the mixture in two parts | see page 35 |.

6   Divide the batter evenly into your prepared cupcake or muffin tray
    and bake for 15 minutes, or until just brown and a toothpick inserted
    in the centre comes out clean. Remove and allow to cool in the tin
    for 10 minutes before transferring to a wire rack to cool completely.

7   Turn the oven up to 200°C/gas mark 8 and make the caramelised
    bacon. Lay the bacon strips out on your prepared baking tray and
    brush with the maple syrup. Bake for 20–25 minutes, or until crispy.
    Cut the bacon into 12 small strips.

8   Pipe the cooled tea cakes with the frosting, then add a toasted pecan
    and a strip of crispy bacon. Add a drizzle of maple syrup and some
    cracked black pepper.

MAPLE FROSTING

60g unsalted butter, room temperature

300g icing sugar, sifted

1 tsp vanilla extract

125ml double cream

4 tbsp maple syrup

Beat the butter alone for 2 minutes until soft, then add the icing sugar, vanilla and double cream, then the maple syrup, beating until smooth and creamy.

PINK GRAPEFRUIT, ALMOND AND BROWN SUGAR TEA CAKES

This recipe uses a variation on the basic frangipane on page 258, but you can substitute either recipe for the other. This one is richer because of the brown sugar, and has a deeper caramel flavour that's lovely with the tart grapefruit.

PREP TIME

25 minutes

COOKING TIME

40 minutes

MAKES: 12

1 pink grapefruit | use half the zest for
   the frangipane, see below |

30g flaked almonds

1 tbsp light brown sugar, for sprinkling

2 tbsp apricot jam | optional |

FOR THE FRANGIPANE SPONGE

150g unsalted butter, room
   temperature

150g light brown sugar

200g ground almonds

Finely grated zest of ½ pink grapefruit

2 eggs

35g plain flour, sifted

One 12-hole cupcake/muffin tray,
   well greased

One baking tray, lined

1 Preheat the oven to 180°C fan assisted/gas mark 6.

2 Top and tail the zested grapefruit and cut away the peel. Using a sharp knife, carefully cut out the fruit segments from just inside the membrane. Discard the membrane and juice, then place the segments on your prepared baking tray and bake for 20 minutes. Remove from the oven, and allow to cool. Leave the oven on.

3 To make the frangipane, beat the butter and sugar together for approximately 3 minutes. Beat in the ground almonds and zest, followed by the eggs and then the flour. Spoon evenly into your prepared cupcake or muffin tray and press a cooled grapefruit segment on top of each. Sprinkle with the flaked almonds and brown sugar.

4 Bake for 20 minutes, or until a cocktail stick inserted into the centre comes out clean.

5 To make the optional glaze, mix the apricot jam with a few drops of water in a heavy-bottomed pan and heat over a medium heat until runny but not bubbling hot. Brush a little of the glaze over each tea cake as they come out of the oven. Allow to cool in the tray for 10 minutes before transferring to a wire rack to cool completely.

BAKED APPLE CIDER DOUGHNUTS

I made these for 180, my cake and cocktail club, to be served during an act in which Marawa the Amazing climbed a ladder of swords barefoot (in green sequin hotpants) and made an apple fruit salad on the blades. I served the doughnuts on mini swords with a glass of champagne.

I use a silicone mini muffin baking tray to make these, but you could just as easily use a doughnut pan, or even just drop them directly onto a lined baking tray (just be aware they will bake into uneven shapes).

PREP TIME

25 minutes

COOKING TIME

20 minutes

MAKES: 12

180g plain flour, sifted

1¾ tsp baking powder

60g light brown sugar

Pinch of sea salt

½ freshly grated nutmeg

75g unsalted butter, cubed and
    refrigerated

60ml whole milk

1 egg

600g cooking apples | 2–3 apples |,
    peeled, cored, cut into 1–2cm
    cubes and steeped overnight
    in 250ml cider with an optional
    cinnamon stick or star anise

FOR THE TOPPING

100g unsalted butter, melted

100g caster sugar

Pinch of ground cinnamon

Pinch of freshly grated nutmeg

One 12-hole silicone mini-muffin tray

1   Preheat the oven to 180°C fan assisted/gas mark 6.

2   In a bowl, whisk together the flour, baking powder, brown sugar, sea salt and nutmeg and set aside. Add the butter and pass it through your fingertips lightly, thumbs across fingers, to make breadcrumbs – the aim here is to coat the flour in the butter, not rub it in, so keep your fingers light and fast. This will take approximately 5 minutes. Alternatively you could use a food processor or a mixer with the paddle attachment for this stage.

3   In another bowl, whisk together the milk and the eggs. Fold into the flour mix | the batter will be wet |.

4   Remove the whole spice from the steeped apples, drain them, discarding the cider, and use kitchen paper to soak up any excess liquid. Fold the apples into the batter.

5   Transfer to your prepared trays and bake for 20 minutes, or until lightly golden brown and risen. Remove from the oven and allow to cool in the trays for 10 minutes. Brush the doughnuts liberally all over with the melted butter, then roll in the combined sugar and spices. Serve immediately.

HACKNEY BUNS AND CHELSEA SMILE BUNS

The Chelsea bun was invented in the eighteenth century at the 'Bun House' in Chelsea, a hot-spot for aristocrats in its time. Our version is the 'Hackney bun', so named for its East London roots and booze-soaked fruit. We also make 'Chelsea Smile buns', invented for an event that traced 'The History of East London in Cake'. Legendary East London gangsters the Krays operated just up the street from our bakery in their day and were notorious for giving their enemies the 'Chelsea Smile'. These buns have blood-soaked (rhubarb coulis) grins and the fruit is soaked in gin – apparently their favourite tipple!

PREP TIME
50 minutes, plus proving times

COOKING TIME
25 minutes

MAKES: 12

200ml whole milk

60g unsalted butter, cubed

450g strong white bread flour, sifted,
    plus extra for kneading

1 tsp salt

50g caster sugar

15g fresh yeast

3 egg yolks

FOR THE FILLING AND TOPPING

50g unsalted butter, melted

100g dark brown sugar

100g sultanas or raisins, soaked
    overnight in 120ml Guinness, then
    drained and syrup reserved

25g Spiced Caster Sugar | see page 228 |

One 25cm square baking tin, lined

NOTE: Soaking the sultanas/raisins not only adds amazing flavour but also saturates them, meaning they will rob very little moisture from the dough, making for a softer bun and a better rise.

1 Heat the milk and butter in a pan over a medium heat, swirling until the butter is melted – don't let it boil. Remove from the heat and leave to cool.

2 In a bowl, whisk together the flour, salt and sugar, mixing thoroughly to distribute the salt. When working with yeast, remember that salt is its enemy – the two should not come directly into contact if you can help it.

3 Whisk the yeast into the cooled butter mixture, then whisk in all the egg yolks evenly. Pour onto the dry ingredients. Mix it all up lightly until you have formed a dough that's sticky but not sloppy. You may need to add little more water or flour to achieve this consistency. Turn the dough out onto an unfloured surface and knead for 20 minutes | see pages 135–136 |. Once you have finished, leave the kneaded dough to rise for 1 hour in a warm place.

4 Turn the dough out onto a floured surface. Roll it evenly into a rectangular shape until it's about 25 x 35cm and 1cm thick. Brush all over with most of the melted butter, then sprinkle all over with the dark brown sugar and drained soaked fruit. Roll the whole thing up lengthways like a big Swiss roll – the tighter the better! Brush some of the remaining butter around the outside, then cut into 12 slices approximately 2cm wide, using a small serrated knife, and place them in rows in your prepared tin, leaving small gaps to allow for a further rise. Prove for 20 minutes | see page 137 |.

5 Preheat the oven to 200°C fan assisted/gas mark 8 and bake for 20–30 minutes, or until golden brown.

6 Remove from the oven and leave to cool in the tin for 10 minutes before transferring to a wire rack. When cooling, brush all over with the leftover Guinness syrup and sprinkle with the spiced caster sugar.

TO MAKE
CHELSEA SMILE BUNS

Make as above, but soak the fruit in gin instead of Guinness. Make up
a batch of rhubarb coulis | see page 256 | and use a squeezy bottle to
mark a smile on each one | or just drizzle it all over |.

BROWN SUGAR BRIOCHE

Brioche is a sweetened French bread enriched with butter and eggs. You can flavour your brioche however you like – in the bakery we make them with cardamom and date, orange and almond, dark chocolate, dried apricot and walnut, pistachio, cinnamon, or dried fruit soaked in Guinness and spices. Brioche is best eaten on the day, but if you make too much you can turn the leftovers into bread and butter pudding | see page 176 |.

PREP TIME

30 minutes, plus chilling, rising and resting times

COOKING TIME

35 minutes

MAKES: 1 loaf

300g plain flour, sifted

40g dark brown sugar

1 tsp salt

15g fresh yeast

50ml cold water

75ml whole milk

5 egg yolks

175g unsalted butter, room temperature, cubed

Egg wash: 1 egg yolk lightly beaten with 25ml double cream or milk

One 500g loaf tin, greased

1   In a large bowl, whisk together the flour, sugar and salt.

2   In another bowl, crumble the yeast into the water, milk and egg yolks and whisk to dissolve and combine. Add this to the dry mixture and combine with your hands, or a spatula or pastry scraper if you have one, until the dough comes together – it will be very sticky at this stage. Cover the surface with clingfilm and leave to rest at room temperature for 20 minutes.

3   Turn out onto a lightly floured surface and knead for 15–20 minutes | see pages 135–136 |. Now add the butter, a few cubes at a time, kneading it into the dough, making sure the butter is incorporated before you add more. Add any flavourings you want to use now. Lightly flour the dough all over and put it back into the bowl. Cover with clingfilm again and refrigerate for 1 hour.

4   Take the dough out, shape it into a loaf approximately 25 x 15cm and place it in your prepared tin, seam facing down. Once this is done, refrigerate for a further hour. Then remove from the fridge and leave to rest at room temperature for 30 minutes.

5   Preheat the oven to 220°C fan assisted/gas mark 9.

6   Brush the dough all over with the egg wash. Turn the oven down to 180°C/gas mark 6 and bake for 35–40 minutes, taking care not to burn the top. You may need to turn the oven down to 150°C/gas mark 5 after 30 minutes if the loaf is starting to over-brown.

7   Remove from the oven and allow to cool in the tin for 10 minutes before transferring to a wire rack to cool completely.

TO MAKE CARDAMOM AND DATE BRIOCHE: After the mixing stage, add the ground seeds of 5 green cardamom pods | use a pestle and mortar or spice grinder | and 10 stoned and chopped dates.

SPICED BRIOCHE POPPY SEED BAGEL

This recipe was developed to celebrate the history of Brick Lane in East London. People have been making the pilgrimage to Brick Lane for bagels since long before it was a hipster postcode. According to one cabbie I met, twenty years ago the only reason anyone would book a cab to that part of town was for 4 a.m. bagels or to get early morning newspapers, as they get dropped there first. This recipe celebrates the rich cultural history of the cuisines of Brick Lane past and present, by combining elements of French Protestant (brioche), the Jewish population (bagel) and the Bangladeshi community (the spice mix and poppy seeds) – all of which have inhabited the area over the years and made it famous for its food.

PREP TIME

1 hour, plus chilling, rising and
   resting times

COOKING TIME

10 minutes

MAKES: 12

⅓ tsp ground cloves

½ tsp ground cardamom seeds

¼ tsp ground cinnamon

⅓ tsp mixed spice

1 batch of uncooked Brioche dough,
   prepared to end of step 3
   | see page 172 |

Egg wash: 1 egg yolk lightly beaten with
   25ml double cream or milk

25g poppy seeds

Two baking trays, lined

1   In a bowl, combine the spices and set aside.

2   Make up the brioche dough, kneading in the spices evenly at step 3 | see page 172 |. Refrigerate the dough as per recipe.

3   Remove the dough from the fridge. Weigh out 60g pieces, roll them into individual balls and place on your prepared tray. Leave for 5 minutes to allow the gluten to relax.

4   Poke a finger through the centre of each ball and work the hole so that you can fit a finger in from each hand, pointing in opposite directions. Then turn one finger over the other in a twiddling motion. Make the hole bigger than you think it needs to be, to allow for the dough stretching back and then swelling during proving.

5   Preheat the oven to 180°C fan assisted/gas mark 6.

6   Brush the bagels with the egg wash, sprinkle with the poppy seeds, then prove | see page 137 | for 15–20 minutes.

7   Bake for 10 minutes, or until the bagels have a nice even golden colour across the top | check for browning on the bottom too |. Remove and allow to cool on the tray for 10 minutes before transferring to a wire rack to cool completely.

BREAD AND BUTTER PUDDING

Bread and butter pudding has been around in Britain for centuries. Early incarnations called for either butter or bone marrow and could be made with bread or rice, but at some point they parted ways to become bread and butter and rice pudding. Originally invented to make use of leftovers, this recipe works best with stale bread – if the bread is too fresh you can end up with a soggy mess.

PREP TIME

10 minutes

COOKING TIME

20 minutes

SERVES: 6

½ batch of Brioche
| see page 172 | sliced

120g raisins

80g unsalted butter, melted

1 batch of Simple Thick Custard,
cooled | see page 261 |

One 20cm square pie dish, greased

1 Preheat the oven to 180°C fan assisted/gas mark 6.

2 Pack the brioche slices tightly into your prepared pie dish. Dot the raisins throughout and brush the brioche all over with the melted butter. Pour in the custard and bake for 20 minutes, or until the custard is starting to set.

VARIATIONS: Try soaking the raisins in rum, brandy or grappa overnight before using, draining off any excess liquid before adding them to your pie dish. Or brush the top of the freshly baked pudding with jam or jelly. We use homemade English grape jelly in the bakery.

MERINGUE

MERINGUE

MERINGUES are made of egg whites and sugar, whipped until stiff, and baked to form crisp shells with a pillow-soft chewy centre. The trick to making meringues is getting the egg whites whipped perfectly, but baking is crucial too – meringues are only very lightly baked, so that the surface is crisp and the insides remain chewy; a long slow bake in a low oven ensures they partly bake and then slowly dry out.

Once you've got the hang of them, meringues are really simple to make and very versatile. You can work them into pavlova, Eton Mess or a pie topping, and dip them into chocolate, crush them into ice cream or pipe them into decorative shapes.

THE EGG FOAM

Meringues have a very delicate structure, the basis of which is an egg 'foam' that is reinforced with sugar. Egg whites produce a good foam when they are beaten and this is what makes them so useful in lifting baked goods – not the egg, but the air it can trap. The stress of the beating causes proteins in the whites to unfold, their bonds loosening; then, just as they relax, they bump into other unwound proteins and form a bond with them, capturing an air bubble as they go, in a flexible little pocket.

Your aim in foaming an egg white is to create lots of small bubbles, so start beating on a low speed or you'll end up beating in big pockets of air. Once you have a foam of small bubbles, the faster you beat the whites the more air is incorporated and the better the whole thing will expand.

EQUIPMENT

A copper or metal bowl is best for whipping egg whites; glass will do too, but plastic is a last resort – oil clings to plastic, and any remaining molecules will prevent the whites from foaming. Oil is your enemy when whipping egg whites, and any traces of fat, grease or dirt will also inhibit the egg from foaming, so you need all your equipment squeaky clean. Rubbing equipment down with a wedge of lemon or lime and then drying will remove all hidden traces of grease.

OVEN TIME

The oven temperature for meringues should be very low – you only want the meringue to bake very slightly, then dry out so it sets. If you're making larger meringues, you can turn off the oven after the baking time and leave the meringues in for another hour or so. The residual heat will continue to set them but won't dry them out too much, so they won't become crumbly and fall apart.

HOW TO WHIP PERFECT MERINGUES

SEPARATE your eggs | see page 20 |, making sure there are no traces of yolk in your whites – yolks contain fat and will prevent the egg whites from foaming properly. Put the whites into your clean, dry bowl and have your mixer ready.

Now, with your mixer on a low speed, start beating the whites. As they start to foam very slightly, add a tiny dash of lemon juice – the acidity of the juice will bring the pH level of the whites down to a point where the proteins can unfold more easily. This stabilises the whites and helps them to reach full volume. (If you don't have any lemon juice, you can use another acid, such as cream of tartar or white wine vinegar.) Gradually increase the speed of your mixer to medium, then to high, until the whites are almost stiff – this is what is called the soft peaks stage.

Now you need to add the sugar – this helps strengthen the egg foam. You need to be careful not to add it too early, or it will inhibit the proteins from forming bonds. It should only be added at this soft peaks stage.

Start adding your sugar very gradually – approximately 2 tablespoons at a time, beating for at least 30 seconds between additions. You are done when the whites form stiff peaks. You can test for stiff peaks by lifting the beater directly upward, out of the bowl – if the beaten whites stand on end and hold their place they are done; if they flop back they are at the soft peaks stage and not ready.

SOFT PEAKS

STIFF PEAKS

NOTE: Be careful not to go too far or you'll break the foam. As the protein bonds increase in number and become tighter, they squeeze out their water content. If you go too far, the bubble walls will dry out and burst, the foam will collapse and it won't rise.

TIP: Holding the bowl at an angle so the liquid is forced up will help to trap more air.

BASIC MERINGUES

Here is a simple meringue recipe which you can use and adapt to make different shapes and flavours. Meringues will keep stored in airtight containers for up to two weeks. Your whites will be very delicate once whipped, so you need to impact them as little as possible and get them into the oven very quickly so that they don't collapse.

PREP TIME

15 minutes

COOKING TIME

1 hour, plus 1 hour cooling in the oven

MAKES: 10

6 large egg whites, room temperature

1 tsp lemon juice

280g caster sugar

One baking tray, lined

1 Preheat the oven to 120°C fan assisted/gas mark 1.

2 In a bowl, whip the egg whites | see page 181 | with the lemon juice until soft peaks form – approximately 5 minutes. Slowly beat in the sugar – 2 tablespoons at a time – and continue until stiff peaks form.

3 Use a piping bag to pipe dollops of the beaten whites onto your prepared baking tray and bake for 1 hour or until set. Turn off the oven and leave the meringues inside to dry for another hour.

TIP: Pipe a dot of meringue in each corner of your baking tray to attach the baking paper – especially handy if you have a fan oven, which might blow your meringues out of place.

TIP: If you are making a huge batch and have an oven full of meringues dehydrating, there will be a lot of moisture in the oven – you may need to slightly increase the temperature about halfway through to eradicate the steam.

MERINGUE BONES

These bones are great for Hallowe'en with a side dish of mixed berry coulis 'blood'.
You can use the same method to pipe almost any shape of meringue you like —
so long as the joins are thick enough to hold together.

PREP TIME

20 minutes

COOKING TIME

1 hour, plus 1 hour cooling time

MAKES: 20

1 batch of uncooked Basic Meringues

| see page 182 |

1 batch of Mixed Berry Coulis

| see page 256 |

One baking tray, lined

1   Preheat the oven to 120°C fan assisted/gas mark 1.

2   Make up a batch of basic meringue and spoon the mix into a piping bag fitted with a #10 tip.

3   Pipe your shapes onto the prepared baking tray – start at the round edge of the bone and work your way down to make the length, then finish on the round of the opposite side. Repeat in reverse to make a crisscross, overlapping your meringue down the length of the bone, and ensuring there are no weak spots where the meringue is too thin and likely to break.

4   Bake for 1 hour, or until set. Turn off the oven and leave the meringues inside to dry for another hour.

5   Remove and serve with the coulis 'blood'.

CANDY FLOSS MERINGUES

I made these candy floss meringues for a jewellery launch event that was themed like a funfair. The display here is made of polystyrene foam covered in paper.

PREP TIME

30 minutes

COOKING TIME

1 hour and **5** minutes,
   plus **1** hour cooling time

MAKES: 10

200g chocolate of your choice, broken
   into pieces

1 batch of Basic Meringues
   | see page 182 |

Lollipop/cake pop sticks

Edible pink lustre spray | optional |

One baking tray, lined

1   Melt the chocolate in a double boiler | see page 196 |. When the meringues are cool, use a stick to gently pierce the base of each one in the centre. Remove and dip the stick in chocolate up to about 2.5cm deep. Reinsert and hold in place for about 30 seconds, until it starts to set. If it feels steady you can transfer it to the fridge or a cool place to set completely.

2   Remove from the fridge and spray the meringues all over with the lustre spray, if using.

COCOA MERINGUES WITH DARK CHOCOLATE AND PISTACHIO

The golden caster sugar in this recipe gives the meringues a deeper caramel flavour. Feel free to experiment with different types of sugar in your meringues – just make sure you use a caster sugar.

PREP TIME

20 minutes

COOKING TIME

1 hour, plus cooling time

MAKES: 20

5 egg whites

1 tsp lemon juice

Pinch of salt

230g golden caster sugar

30g cocoa powder, sifted

150g dark chocolate

| minimum 70% cocoa solids |
broken into pieces

80g pistachios, ground with a pestle and mortar or roughly chopped until fine but not powdery

One baking tray, lined

1 Preheat the oven to 120°C fan assisted/gas mark 1.

2 In a bowl, whip the egg whites | see page 181 | with the lemon juice and salt until soft peaks form. Slowly beat in the sugar – 2 tablespoons at a time – and continue until stiff peaks form. Fold in the cocoa powder, using a metal spoon or spatula.

3 Using a metal dessert spoon or a piping bag with the 1M nozzle | a 1.5cm open star nozzle | attached, transfer 20 neat dollops of meringue onto your baking tray.

4 Bake for 1 hour, or until set, then turn off the oven and leave the meringues inside to dry for another hour.

5 When cool, melt the chocolate in a double boiler | see page 196 | and very carefully dip the base of each meringue first in the chocolate, then in the crushed pistachio. Alternatively, use a teaspoon to zig-zag chocolate across the top of each meringue and dust with pistachio.

MERINGUE MUSHROOMS

Another ingenious use for the humble meringue – these can look very realistic.
Try decorating a cake with them – attach them to the top with some melted chocolate
and surround with cocoa powder 'soil'.

PREP TIME

20 minutes

COOKING TIME

1 hour, plus 1 hour cooling in the oven

MAKES: 20

5 egg whites

1 tsp lemon juice

Pinch of salt

230g caster sugar

30g cocoa powder, sifted, plus extra for dusting

100g chocolate of your choice, broken into pieces

One baking tray, lined

1 Preheat the oven to 120°C fan assisted/gas mark 1.

2 In a bowl, whip the egg whites | see page 181 | with the lemon juice and salt until soft peaks form. Slowly beat in the sugar – 2 tablespoons at a time – and continue until stiff peaks form. Split the mix in two and fold in two-thirds of the cocoa powder in one half | for the mushroom tops | and the remaining cocoa powder into the other half of the mix | for the mushroom stems |.

3 Using a piping bag with a round tip, pipe the beaten whites onto your prepared tray in short lines to make your mushroom stems, ensuring they are wide enough at the bottom and straight enough to have some stability.

4 Once you have piped out your bases, pipe an equal number of domed rounds to form the tops of your mushrooms.

5 Bake for 1 hour, or until set, then turn off the oven and leave the meringues inside to dry for another hour.

6 Melt the chocolate in a double boiler | see page 196 | and use a dab of the melted chocolate to attach the stems of the mushrooms to the tops. You may need to very gently slice the tip of the base away to leave a flat edge. Dust the mushrooms with more cocoa.

SPRING ETON MESS WITH RHUBARB COULIS AND ELDERFLOWER CREAM

Eton Mess was traditionally served at Eton College's annual cricket game against Winchester College, and has been around since the nineteenth century. Originally it was made with bananas, strawberries and cream or ice cream, but it is now generally served with just strawberries and cream. It's very open to adaptation, so feel free to make it however you like. You can use plain whipped cream in place of the elderflower cream used here.

PREP TIME

1 hour

COOKING TIME

3 hours

SERVES: 8

2 kiwis, peeled and roughly chopped

150g strawberries, hulled and halved

75g blackberries

Flesh of 2 passionfruit

Handful of cherries

1 batch of Rhubarb Coulis or Mixed Berry Coulis | see page 256 |, cooled

FOR THE MERINGUE

4 egg whites

1 tsp lemon juice

200g caster sugar

½ tsp vanilla extract

FOR THE ELDERFLOWER CREAM

400ml double cream

50g icing sugar, sifted

4 tbsp elderflower cordial

One baking tray, lined

1 Preheat the oven to 120°C fan assisted/gas mark 1.

2 In a bowl, whip the egg whites | see page 181 | with the lemon juice until soft peaks form. Slowly beat in the sugar – 2 tablespoons at a time – and continue until stiff peaks form.

3 Beat in the vanilla. Use a metal spoon to dollop 4 large spoonfuls of the beaten whites onto your prepared baking tray, and bake until almost completely dry but still slightly chewy in the centre – approximately 3 hours. Remove from the oven and leave to cool.

4 When ready to serve, whip the cream with the icing sugar and elderflower cordial until it forms soft swirls. Carefully break apart the cooled meringues with your hands. Gently fold together the crushed meringues, fruit and cream, and drizzle generously with the coulis. Serve immediately.

CHOCOLATE

COFFEE AND PECAN TRUFFLES 198 • WHISKY TRUFFLES 200 • GANACHE TARTS WITH HONEYCOMB 202 • POPPING CANDY 'FOOL'S GOLD' CHOCOLATES 205 • ABSINTHE HOT CHOCOLATE 206 • CHOCOLATE SHARDS 209 • CHOCOLATE SHAPES 209 • CHOCOLATE DIPPED FRUITS 209

CHOCOLATE

CHOCOLATE has been around for almost 4,000 years, and historians claim to have found evidence of cacao drinks dating as far back as 1900 BC. Theories as to its origin vary, but it's clear that chocolate has been cherished by many cultures and has a very rich history. In ancient Latin America cacao beans were deemed valuable enough to be used as currency. The Mayans and the Aztecs revered it as holy and assigned it divine and magical properties; they called it the Food of the Gods and believed that wisdom and power resulted from eating it. The Aztecs even claimed that it was their god Quetzalcoatl who stole the cacao plant from paradise and brought it to Earth on the beam of a morning star.

Legend has it that Europeans discovered chocolate when an Aztec king mistook a Spanish explorer for a deity and greeted him with a banquet that included a cacao drink. Until this point in time chocolate is thought to have been served only as a bitter beverage, and it was the Spanish who finally sweetened it in the 1500s – adding spices, vanilla, honey and sugar. From Spain it eventually spread throughout Europe as a much-coveted and fashionable drink. In 1674 a French-owned coffee house in London began to bake with chocolate, including it in their cakes and rolls.

In the last century innovations in chocolate have been made very widely and cheaply – with a whole range of sugar and additives and increasingly less cacao – but in the last ten years purer chocolate has experienced a revival and there are more quality, fair-trade chocolates available to eat and to bake with today.

CHOOSING A CHOCOLATE TO BAKE WITH

Dark chocolate with no added sugar is best for most baking recipes. Look for a chocolate that has a minimum of 70% cocoa solids, and is of good quality, with nice flavour and a silky texture. Try out a few different ones and see what you like best. Don't use chocolate that has vegetable fat listed as an ingredient, and choose a chocolate that you would enjoy eating on its own. Some brands I like include Valrhona, Original Beans, Guittard, Callebaut, Divine and Green & Black's.

USING A DOUBLE BOILER (BAIN-MARIE)

Many of the recipes in this book call for you to heat chocolate, cream and other sauces very carefully, and putting them into a pan on the stove over direct heat doesn't allow you to control the heat transfer enough. A double boiler, otherwise known as a bain-marie, will help you control the temperature better and stop chocolate and sauces like a custard 'splitting', sticking or burning by removing them from direct heat. You don't need any special equipment to make a double boiler – you can make one by putting a metal or heatproof glass bowl that fits snugly over a pan of simmering water. Here's how you do it:

Set your bowl over your pan of simmering water, making sure the bowl doesn't touch the water in the pan – whatever is in the bowl will be heated by the steam trapped in the pan, which will never exceed 100°C (the boiling temperature of water) rather than by being blasted by the direct heat under your pan. When you have finished, always make sure you dry the bottom of the bowl before you tip anything out of it so that you don't spill water into whatever you're making and spoil it.

NOTE: Always melt chocolate slowly on a very low heat, stirring continuously. Follow the directions for each recipe for specifics.

BLOOMING

If your chocolate comes up in worrying grey streaks after heating and cooling, this is called 'blooming' and doesn't mean your chocolate is spoiled, it has simply 'lost its temper' | see below |. Blooming occurs when heating the chocolate causes it to lose its emulsion, separating out the cocoa fat. If this happens, don't panic – you can melt the chocolate down and re-use it. Blooming can be avoided by correctly tempering the chocolate | see below |.

TEMPERING

Controlling the temperature at which you melt chocolate to ensure an even crystallisation of cocoa butter as it solidifies is called 'tempering'. It can be a slightly complicated and painstaking process that takes getting the hang of, and if you are going to be doing a lot of chocolate work, it's worth buying a thermometer and reading up on how to do this properly. However, you can get by with all the chocolate handling needed for the recipes in this book by making sure you follow the advice carefully on each recipe, and by using the 'lip test' to determine when your chocolate is ready | see below |.

THE 'LIP TEST'

This is a handy trick taught to me by one of my bakers, who learnt it from his uncle who was a pâtissier at Fortnum & Mason's for many years. Dip a finger in the melted chocolate and touch it to your lip to check its temperature. When it's ready it should feel slightly cool – the lip is very sensitive and will register the temperature better than on your finger, and if it's cool it means it's just below your body temperature (37°C) and about right. If it feels hot it will likely be over 40°C and still too hot to use. Reduce the temperature by adding some small pieces of chopped chocolate and stirring to melt them.

COFFEE AND PECAN TRUFFLES

These simple truffle recipes can easily be adapted to suit your own tastes – try infusing different flavours into the ganache, or using different toasted nuts. Truffles will keep in an airtight container in the fridge for 3–4 days. I used edible lustre dusts to decorate these – painted onto cacao nibs, toasted almonds and shards of chocolate, which are easily attached with a dab of melted chocolate. In the past, I've also used a sprinkling of salt flakes, edible flowers, powdered spices and a drizzle of white chocolate. Have a look around the kitchen and see what comes to hand.

PREP TIME

25 minutes, plus cooling and chilling times

COOKING TIME

10 minutes

MAKES: 20-25

260g pecans, toasted | see page 257 |

FOR THE GANACHE

250g dark chocolate

| minimum 70% cocoa solids |

broken into pieces

20g unsalted butter, cubed

250ml double cream

3 tbsp very strong espresso

FOR THE COATING

250g dark chocolate

| minimum 70% cocoa solids |

broken into pieces

One baking tray, lined

1 Allow your toasted pecans to cool completely, then reserve some of the nicest ones to use whole. Roughly chop the rest into pieces fine enough to use as a coating.

2 Make the ganache, using the quantities listed on the left and the method on page 259, adding the coffee to the bowl with the chocolate before you put it on the heat. Pour the mixture into your prepared baking tray, ideally so it sits about 2.5cm deep. Refrigerate to set for 30 minutes to 1 hour. Keep an eye on it – you want it to remain malleable and not go rock solid.

3 Remove from the fridge and use a teaspoon to scoop out balls of ganache – round them with your hands as neatly or roughly as you like and place them on a freshly lined baking tray. Return to the fridge for a further 15 minutes or until set a little firmer.

4 To make the coating, place the remaining chocolate in a double boiler | see page 196 | to melt. Remove from the heat when the chocolate is almost melted and stir to melt the rest. Use the 'lip test' | see page 197 | to determine when the temperature is just below body temperature.

5 Drop the firm truffles into the melted chocolate, use a teaspoon to coat, then remove them, allowing any excess chocolate to run off. Roll the truffles in the crushed pecans immediately, then push a whole pecan into the top before the chocolate has time to set. Transfer onto a baking tray lined with a fresh sheet of paper and leave to cool and set at room temperature.

WHISKY TRUFFLES

This whisky burnt butter chocolate ganache is absolutely delicious and shouldn't be restricted to this recipe only – try it in a sweet pastry or chocolate tart case | see page 112 for recipes |.

PREP TIME

40 minutes, plus cooling and chilling times

COOKING TIME

5 minutes

MAKES: 28

FOR THE GANACHE

80g unsalted butter, cubed

200ml double cream

280g dark chocolate

| minimum 70% cocoa solids | broken into pieces

3 tbsp Laphroaig, or any other whisky you like

FOR THE COATING

220g dark chocolate

| minimum 70% cocoa solids | broken into pieces

One baking tray, lined

1   Make the burnt butter. Melt the butter in a heavy-bottomed pan over a medium-high heat for 2 minutes, stirring constantly until it has a dark tan colour | it shouldn't get dark brown or black |. Remove from the heat and set aside to cool completely.

2   Make the ganache, using the quantities listed on the left and the method on page 259, and whisking in the whisky at the final stage. Pour the mixture into your prepared baking tray, ideally so it sits about 2.5cm deep. Refrigerate to set for 30 minutes to 1 hour. Keep an eye on it – you want it to remain malleable and not go rock solid.

3   Remove from the fridge and use a teaspoon to scoop out balls of ganache – round them with your hands as neatly or roughly as you like and place them on a freshly lined baking tray. Return to the fridge for a further 15 minutes, or until set a little firmer.

4   To make the coating, place the remaining chocolate in a double boiler | see page 196 | to melt. Remove from the heat when the chocolate is almost melted and stir to melt the rest. Use the 'lip test' | see page 197 | to determine when the temperature is just below body temperature.

5   Drop the firm truffles into the chocolate, use a teaspoon to coat, then remove them, allowing any excess chocolate to run off. Transfer onto a baking tray lined with a fresh sheet of paper and leave to cool and set at room temperature.

AN IDEA FOR DECORATION

Follow the instructions for Chocolate Shards on page 209. Break up into little shards and attach to each truffle, using a dab of melted chocolate. Paint with lustre dust or leave as they are.

GANACHE TARTS WITH HONEYCOMB

These tarts are very sweet and indulgent, but irresistible when you see them glistening on the cake stand. So be warned…

PREP TIME

1 hour

COOKING TIME

35 minutes

MAKES: 12

1 batch of Sweet or Savoury Shortcrust
Pastry | see pages 100–101 |

Egg wash: 1 egg yolk lightly beaten with
25ml double cream or milk

1 batch of Ganache Filling
| see page 259 |

1 batch of Honeycomb, broken into
small pieces | see page 233 |

One 12-hole cupcake/muffin tray

1 Preheat the oven to 180°C fan assisted/gas mark 6.

2 Roll out the pastry to about 3mm thickness and cut rounds to fit your prepared cupcake/muffin tray, allowing extra to cover the sides – approximately 10cm rounds for a standard cupcake tray. Press these carefully into the cavities and refrigerate for around 30 minutes. Line, weigh down with baking beans and blind bake | see page 98 | for around 10–15 minutes, or until starting to brown. Remove from the oven, brush all over with the egg wash and bake another 2 minutes to seal. Remove and allow to cool.

3 Spoon the ganache evenly into the cooled pastry cases while it's cool but still liquid | use the 'lip test' – see page 197 |. Leave to set completely – approximately 1 hour | you can put them into the fridge to speed this up | before garnishing with the honeycomb.

VARIATIONS: This tart is very versatile – try putting an Earl Grey tea bag in with the cream as it heats up | remove it before you add the chocolate |. Or flavouring with chai, dusting the finished tart with pistachios or topping with fresh berries.

POPPING CANDY 'FOOL'S GOLD' CHOCOLATES

These make great canapés or show-off snacks. The popping candy's 'pop' is cleverly preserved by coating it in melted chocolate – this prevents any liquid, heat or friction from getting to it and setting it off. You can make these with milk or dark chocolate, and use different nuts if almonds are not to your taste.

PREP TIME

20 minutes, plus chilling time

COOKING TIME

5 minutes

MAKES: 20

30g flaked almonds, toasted | optional –
  see page 257 |

600g milk or dark chocolate
  | minimum 70% cocoa solids |
  broken into pieces

3 x 5g sachets of popping candy

½ vial of gold lustre dust

Clean paintbrush | optional |

One baking tray, lined

One cake tin or deep baking tray, lined

1 Melt the chocolate in a double boiler | see page 196 | over a low heat. Remove from the heat when the chocolate is almost melted and stir to melt the rest. Use the 'lip test' | see page 197 | to determine when the temperature is just below body temperature.

2 Roughly chop the nuts, or break up flaked almonds lightly with your hand. Fold these and the popping candy into the cooled | but still liquid | chocolate.

3 Pour the mixture into your prepared cake tin or deep baking tray and refrigerate for 20–30 minutes, or until just starting to firm up but still malleable.

4 Remove from the fridge, use a spoon to scoop out little chunks of the chocolate and shape with your hands into 20 or so rough little 'rocks'. Place on a freshly lined baking tray and return to the fridge to set completely.

5 Remove and coat each chocolate rock with the lustre dust. The quickest, easiest way to do this is to stir the chocolate rocks with a paintbrush in a small bowl containing the dust – this way it will coat from all angles more thickly and evenly than if you attempt to paint it on.

NOTE: Make sure you use a new paintbrush, or one that's only ever been used for food.

ABSINTHE HOT CHOCOLATE

I decided to make this drink the first time I did a night market. It was Christmas time and I knew I would need something substantial (and heady) to keep my temperature and spirits high. We served it with spiced gingerbread | see page 144 for recipe |. Keep in the fridge for up to 3 days, and reheat when needed. For when mulled wine won't cut it …

PREP TIME

10 minutes

COOKING TIME

5 minutes

SERVES: 2-3

400g dark chocolate

| minimum 70% cocoa solids |

broken into pieces

60ml double cream

60ml whole milk

Pinch of sea salt

100ml absinthe

1　Place the chocolate in a medium metal bowl and set aside.

2　Heat the cream and milk in a pan over a medium/low heat until just starting to bubble at the sides | not boiling but getting there |. Then slowly pour the hot cream over the chocolate and leave to sit for 1–2 minutes.

3　Sprinkle in the salt and whisk gently to bring it together. Pour the mixture back into the pan, return to the heat and add the absinthe. Stir over the heat for a minute or two before serving hot.

CHOCOLATE DECORATIONS

These beautiful chocolate decorations, simple and quick to prepare, will
make any cake or tart look spectacular in one simple move. Use them
just on top of a cake, or attach them all over with a layer of buttercream
| see pages 254–255 for recipes |.

CHOCOLATE SHARDS

200g dark chocolate

| minimum 70% cocoa solids |

broken into pieces

½ tsp unsalted butter

Baking paper

TIP: Make sure you dry the bottom of the bowl after removing it from the double boiler, otherwise you might end up spilling water into your chocolate.

1 Melt the chocolate and butter in a double boiler | see page 196 | over a medium heat. Remove from the heat when about two-thirds melted, and stir to melt the remaining chocolate.

2 Using a palette knife, spread the chocolate over a piece of baking paper until it forms a thin sheet | not so thin you can see through it |. Place another piece of paper over the top and smooth out any air pockets. Gently roll the sheets up into a cylinder and place in the fridge to set completely – approximately 1 hour. When you unroll it the chocolate will crack and form your shards.

TO MAKE POPPING CANDY CHOCOLATE SHARDS: Allow the melted chocolate to cool | use the 'lip test' – see page 197 | and gently fold in 2 x 5g packets of popping candy | the fat in the chocolate will seal it in and stop it 'popping' | before you spread it on the baking paper.

CHOCOLATE SHAPES

200g dark chocolate

| minimum 70% cocoa solids |

broken into pieces

½ tsp unsalted butter

Baking paper

One baking tray, lined

1 Follow steps 1 and 2 above but instead of rolling the sheets up into a cylinder, gently roll over the sheets with a rolling pin | taking care to avoid chocolate spilling out of the sides |.

2 Allow to set at room temperature until all the chocolate is firm, then remove the paper. Use a biscuit cutter to cut shapes and transfer them to your prepared baking tray. Store in the fridge until ready to use.

CHOCOLATE DIPPED FRUITS

200g dark chocolate

| minimum 70% cocoa solids |

broken into pieces

250g fresh fruit – strawberries, raspberries and physalis work well

One baking tray, lined

1 Melt the chocolate in a double boiler | see page 196 | over a medium heat. Remove from the heat when about two-thirds melted and stir to melt the remaining chocolate. Use the 'lip test' | see page 197 | to determine when the temperature is just below body temperature.

2 Dip the fruit in the melted chocolate and place on your prepared baking tray to set at room temperature.

SUGAR

SUGAR

CANDY making has its origins in medicine. In medieval times apothecaries used sugary goodness to administer their remedies, but the practice soon spread and by the 1600s hard candies were common fare.

For beginners: there's nothing scary about working with sugar – you must be extra careful, as it often means working with hot, sticky liquids, but if you stick to the recipe and instructions you'll be fine.

Specific temperatures are often required, so use a sugar thermometer and the chart opposite. You will also need a heavy-bottomed pan, baking paper and a heatproof silicone spatula.

A NOTE ON CLEANING UP

After making candy, your thermometer and pan will be covered in cooled rock-hard sugar syrup, but don't worry. It will easily come off if you fill the pan with water and return it to the stove until it dissolves.

MAKING SUGAR SYRUPS

When you heat sugar and water together, the sugar liquefies and they form a syrup. This syrup can then be used on its own or to form the basis of various candies.

CRYSTALLISATION

Once liquefied, sugar (sucrose) molecules will attempt to re-form themselves into solid crystals, creating clumps around the inside of your pan. This is called crystallisation and is something you want to avoid in most cases.

TOP TIPS FOR PREVENTING CRYSTALLISATION

- Adding a sugar other than sucrose – such as liquid glucose – will stop the sucrose molecules re-attaching (imagine Lego bricks trying to fit together when there are other pieces that don't fit getting in the way).
- Adding an acid such as lemon juice or cream of tartar to the mix will cause some of the sucrose to break up (or invert) into its two simpler components, fructose and glucose, which again, get in the way of crystals forming.
- Make sure there are no sugar crystals (or 'seed' crystals) stuck to the side of the pan, as these will attract others and form bigger crystals. Brush them away with a (clean) moistened pastry brush.
- Avoid any particles of dust or scratches in the pan that can attract crystal nuclei, which will again attract other crystals.
- Avoid agitating the solution at any stage by taking the following precautions:
  - * Clamp the thermometer to the side of the pan and avoid moving it.
  - * Pour the syrup from the pan (don't scrape).
  - * Don't tilt or jolt the pan.

HOW TO USE A SUGAR THERMOMETER

A SUGAR thermometer is very useful in candy making – it clamps on to the inside of the pan and can read up to very high temperatures. For best results you should test your thermometer before you first use it (and from time to time to check that it's accurate). Leave it in a pan of boiling water for 10 minutes – the reading should be 100°C. If it's not, adapt your reading of the thermometer accordingly when you use it. Another tip for good results is to ensure that the thermometer does not touch the base of your pan – it's the temperature of the sugar you need to know, not that of the pan.

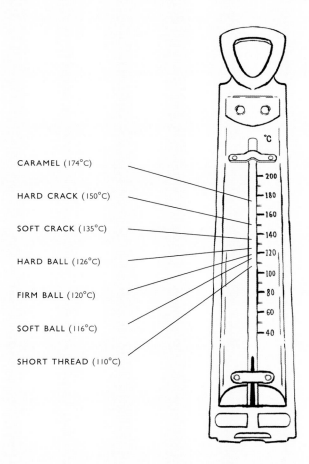

CARAMEL (174°C)

HARD CRACK (150°C)

SOFT CRACK (135°C)

HARD BALL (126°C)

FIRM BALL (120°C)

SOFT BALL (116°C)

SHORT THREAD (110°C)

Before candy thermometers were invented, confectioners tested various stages of sugar making by dropping a dab of the syrup into a bowl of cold water – the sugar would react differently at each stage. The illustration above lists the various stages and their corresponding temperatures – it's a handy converter in case you come across a recipe that uses these terms as a guideline, or if you don't have a thermometer.

The 'short thread' stage is tested by cooling a little bit of syrup, then pulling it between the thumb and forefinger – if the correct stage has been reached, a thread will form. For all the other stages, a small dab of the syrup is dropped into cold water. A smooth lump indicates 'ball' stages, at various degrees of hardness as described. At the 'soft crack' stage, the syrup forms threads that are still pliable. At the 'hard crack' stage, the threads are brittle.

PECAN BRITTLE

Pecan brittle can be eaten on its own or used as a garnish for ice creams, cakes and tarts. The little bit of baking soda in this recipe makes the brittle lighter and easier on the crunch, leaving it somewhere between a brittle and a honeycomb. Read the tips on working with sugar on page 212 before you begin.

PREP TIME

15 minutes

COOKING TIME

15 minutes

MAKES: 500g

210g caster sugar

125ml water

125ml liquid glucose

1 tbsp lemon juice

Pinch of sea salt

300g pecans, toasted | see page 257 |

1 tsp bicarbonate of soda

Sugar thermometer

One baking tray, lined

1   Put the sugar, water, liquid glucose, lemon juice and salt into a medium-sized heavy-bottomed pan with a sugar thermometer attached and stir to combine.

2   Turn the heat on to medium high and leave the mixture alone. Watch the thermometer, and when it reaches the hard ball stage – 120°C, approximately 5 minutes – add the nuts, stir to coat and continue to cook until your mixture is a deep brown colour – around 150°C, approximately 5 minutes.

3   Remove from the heat, stir in the bicarbonate of soda and immediately pour out onto your prepared baking tray. It will foam up and get everywhere if you're not careful – it's also very hot, so mind you don't burn yourself. When cool, crack into pieces and enjoy.

BLANCHED PECANS

A lovely garnish for ice cream, pies, crumble or coffee cakes. Use crushed or whole.
Will keep stored in an airtight container for a week.

PREP TIME

5 minutes

COOKING TIME

15 minutes

60g pecans

15g icing sugar

One baking tray, lined

1 Preheat the oven to 180°C fan assisted/gas mark 6.

2 Rinse the pecans in cold water and drain. Transfer them to a clean bowl, sift the icing sugar over the top and stir quickly to coat them as evenly as you can.

3 Transfer to your prepared baking tray and bake for 15 minutes, turning occasionally by tossing the tray. Tip onto a plate to cool.

CANDIED NUTS

Use as a garnish, add to a crumble | see page 128 | or serve over ice cream | see page 241 |. Use whichever nuts you like best. If you prefer to use chopped nuts, toast them first and you'll find they're much easier to chop.

PREP TIME

5 minutes

COOKING TIME

20 minutes

MAKES: 250g

150g nuts of your choice

150g caster sugar

¼ tsp sea salt

One baking tray, lined

1   Preheat the oven to 200°C fan assisted/gas mark 8.

2   Spread the nuts on your prepared baking tray and bake for 5–10 minutes, or until aromatic and just starting to brown. Remove from the oven and leave to cool | transferring them onto a cold plate or surface will speed this up |.

3   Place the sugar in a medium-sized heavy-bottomed pan over a medium heat, stirring with a wooden spoon until it begins to liquefy. Keep stirring until all the sugar has liquefied and turned a medium amber colour.

4   Now quickly add the nuts to the pan, stirring to evenly coat each one. Once coated, spread them out on a freshly lined baking tray, using a fork to separate any conjoined nuts. Sprinkle with salt and leave to cool completely.

APPLES AND PEARS 'JACK THE RIPPER' FRUIT LEATHER APRONS

Jack the Ripper was nicknamed 'Leather Apron' by the press after a scrap of bloodstained leather was found near the scene of one of his grisly murders. Our bakery is just up the road from where the murders took place and, rather morbidly, we made this fruit leather for a project which documented 'The History of East London in Cake'. The strawberry coulis makes for a lovely bloodstain! Keeps stored airtight in a cool dry place for up to three months.

PREP TIME

15 minutes

COOKING TIME

12 hours

750g mix of Bramley apples and pears, peeled, cored and cut into small chunks

2 tbsp brown sugar

Juice of 1 lemon

1 tbsp olive oil

½ batch of Strawberry Coulis
| optional – see page 256 |

Two small baking trays, lined

1   Preheat the oven to 60°C fan assisted/lowest possible gas temperature.

2   Put the fruit, brown sugar and lemon juice into a heavy-bottomed pan, cover and cook gently until softened enough to purée – approximately 20 minutes. Remove from the heat and purée using a hand mixer, a food processor or by forcing the fruit through a wide mesh metal sieve with the back of a ladle. Stir in the olive oil.

3   Spread the fruit in your prepared baking trays and smooth to the edges. The fruit layers should be approximately 4–5mm thick.

4   Bake overnight, for 12 hours, until completely dry and the fruit peels away easily from the baking paper. Once cool, tear or cut into strips and drizzle over the strawberry coulis if using.

WHISKY SALT CARAMEL POPCORN

I made this caramel popcorn as a canapé for a Dom Perignon launch party. Originally it had caraway seeds in it, but sometime around Christmas they were replaced with whisky (as are a lot of things). The added baking soda and long exposure to a low heat lightens the caramel to a crisp crunch, so it's not so heavy and doesn't stick in your teeth the way caramel does. Experiment with different flavours such as the original caraway seeds, or vanilla, or substitute cognac for the whisky. Make sure you make more than you need, as this recipe comes with a high snack warning.

PREP TIME

15 minutes

COOKING TIME

1 hour

MAKES: 350g

1 tbsp vegetable oil

120g popcorn maize

120g light brown sugar

Generous pinch of sea salt

110g unsalted butter, room
    temperature

60g liquid glucose

130ml Laphroaig, or any other whisky
    you like

2 tsp bicarbonate of soda

Two baking trays, lined

1 Preheat the oven to 100°C fan assisted/gas mark ¼.

2 Heat the vegetable oil in a large pan. Add the maize, cover and heat gently. Shake the pan and wait to hear the corn popping. Once it has all popped – 4–5 minutes – remove any unpopped corn, transfer the popped corn to a metal or glass bowl and set aside.

3 Put the sugar, salt, butter and liquid glucose into a heavy-bottomed pan over a low heat. Stir slowly with a wooden spoon to gently incorporate everything as the butter melts and the sugar dissolves. Once the sugar has dissolved, turn the temperature up high and heat for 3 minutes. Add the whisky and heat for another 2 minutes. Then remove from the heat and add the bicarbonate of soda.

4 Spoon the caramel over the popped corn so it's lightly and evenly coated. Transfer to your prepared baking trays and bake for 45 minutes to 1 hour, or until slightly puffed – it should be light and crispy, so if it's not quite ready, return it to the oven for a little longer.

5 Remove and allow to cool a little before breaking apart into small clusters.

HARD CANDY 'JEWELS'

Moulding boiled sugar will give you realistic-looking 'jewels' that are great for decorating. Made this way, candy is hygroscopic (absorbs liquid) so it will melt over time, especially if there's moisture in the air. I once made a pile of jewels for a marzipan dragon to sit on outside a cake castle for kids at Camp Bestival, but they melted in the humidity, so in the end he was sitting in a pile of lava. You can buy food-safe silicone moulds to make these jewel shapes in cake shops or online. A few drops of food colouring are used to colour the jewels – you'll need to make multiple batches if you want different-coloured jewels. See notes at the beginning of this chapter | page 212 | on preventing sugar crystallisation.

PREP TIME

10 minutes

COOKING TIME

10 minutes, plus cooling time

MAKES: 20–25

205g caster sugar
80ml liquid glucose
A few drops of gel food colouring
4fl oz water

Sugar thermometer
Silicone jewel moulds

1   Place the sugar, glucose syrup, food colouring and water in a pan with a sugar thermometer attached and stir to combine. Heat over a medium heat to 150°C without stirring.

2   Remove from the heat and let the mixture cool to 130°C.

3   Pour into a heatproof glass jug, then pour carefully into your moulds, avoiding scraping the pan. The candy will start to harden as soon as it's away from the heat, and will speed up if you try to spoon it into the moulds, so work quickly. If you have any leftover candy you can pour it onto a lined baking sheet to make sugar glass | see page 225 |. Allow to cool until completely set.

SUGAR SHARDS

Sugar glass is what they use in films whenever you see glass being smashed – it's hard and transparent, more brittle than glass (and less dangerous). Because sugar glass is hygroscopic, you should smash it into shards soon after it is fully cooled or it will start to absorb liquid and soften, losing its brittle quality. If you want to make different-coloured sugar shards, you will need to make a fresh batch for each one – don't try to split the mix and colour it separately, as you have to work quickly with the liquid before it sets.

PREP TIME

10 minutes

COOKING TIME

25 minutes

MAKES: 800g

500ml water

785g granulated sugar

A few drops of gel food colouring

| optional |

250ml liquid glucose

¼ tsp cream of tartar

One shallow baking tray, lined with foil, with no gaps

Oil spray

Sugar thermometer

1   Spray your prepared baking tray all over with the oil spray at least 30 minutes before you want to use it.

2   Place the water, sugar, food colouring | if using |, liquid glucose and cream of tartar into a pan with a sugar thermometer attached and stir to combine. Bring to the boil over a medium heat, until it reaches 150°C – approximately 15 minutes.

3   Remove from the heat and let the mixture cool to 130°C – approximately 10 minutes – then pour the mixture quickly and carefully into the oiled baking tray. Allow to cool completely.

4   Pop the sugar sheet very carefully out of the tray, then, using a meat tenderiser, hit the sheet carefully in the centre so it cracks into shards.

TIP: You can use a sharp knife to score the sugar glass before cracking it.

CANDIED ORANGE SLICES

These make a good garnish, especially for chocolate cakes and tarts. You can use blood oranges if you can get hold of them – they will take slightly longer on the stove.

PREP TIME

5 minutes

COOKING TIME

1 hour

300ml water

125g caster or granulated sugar

2 oranges, topped and tailed and cut
   into thin round slices

1   Place the water, sugar and orange slices in a heavy-bottomed pan over a medium heat until the peel starts to look translucent – about 40 minutes to 1 hour.

2   Remove from the heat and store on baking paper until ready to use.

CANDIED LIMES

PREP TIME

5 minutes

COOKING TIME

20 minutes

3 limes, topped and tailed and cut into
   thin round slices

100g caster or granulated sugar, plus
   optional extra for dusting

100ml water

1   First, bring a pan of water to the boil and blanch the limes by placing them in the boiling water for 5 minutes. Drain and set aside.

2   In another pan, bring the sugar and water to the boil over a high heat. Add the limes and simmer for 12 minutes, or until the white pith turns translucent and the limes look candied and shiny. Drain and allow to cool.

3   Coat the finished limes in a dusting of sugar if you like, and store in an airtight container, separated with baking paper.

VANILLA SUGAR

Flavoured sugars can be used as an ingredient or for sprinkling over buns and shortbreads. My grandmother was a great baker and always kept a jar of vanilla sugar in her larder – when I was a small child I thought it was just about the most exotic thing you could have.

1 vanilla pod
1 x 500g jar of granulated or caster sugar

Drop the vanilla pod into the jar of sugar and leave it to work its magic. Alternatively, pulse the pod and seeds in a food mixer, or chop very finely and shake in the jar to distribute evenly.

SPICED SUGAR

1 tsp mixed spice
1 tsp ground cinnamon
4 cloves
1 x 200g jar of granulated or caster sugar

Stir the spices through the sugar and shake to distribute evenly. Remove the cloves before using.

CARAMELISED ORANGE SLICES

A very handy and simple recipe, these oranges make a delicious bitter-sweet snack with natural yoghurt or ice cream and can be used in so many desserts and pies. In the bakery we use them to top our winter Bakewells, custard tarts | see page 120 | trifles and chocolate cakes. You can use the same method to caramelise lemons and limes too — just adjust the amount of sugar slightly to balance the extra bitterness. They will keep stored in an airtight container in the fridge for 3 days.

PREP TIME

15 minutes

COOKING TIME

10 minutes

3 oranges, topped and tailed and peel
 cut away
100g caster sugar

1 With a sharp knife carefully cut out the segments of the oranges just inside the membrane | skin of the segment |. Put them on a plate and set aside.

2 Squeeze the juice from the pulpy leftover chunk in the centre of the orange into a glass and reserve.

3 Place the sugar in a heavy-bottomed pan over a medium heat. Avoid stirring it while it heats up, but shake the pan from time to time to prevent it from sticking. The sugar will melt and caramelise quite quickly after about 5–6 minutes, so watch it carefully. As soon as the sugar is fully melted and a dark amber colour, remove the pan from the heat and stir in the reserved orange juice to stop it cooking. Let it cool completely before adding the orange segments and stirring to combine.

CRYSTALLISED FLOWERS

You should only eat flowers that are grown without chemical pesticides, which unfortunately rules out most of the flowers you can get hold of unless you grow your own or order them online. I love the mild, fresh flavour of pansies and violas. Crystallised flowers look really beautiful on top of a finished cake or fairy cake, and can even be baked into the tops of sugar cookies. Make sure your workspace isn't too hot or humid before you start. If you're careful to make sure the whole flower is coated, these little beauties will keep stored airtight for up to a year.

PREP TIME

10 minutes, plus drying time

Handful of edible flowers

1–2 egg whites, loosened with a few drops of water | approximately 4 drops per white |

Small bowl of caster sugar

One baking tray, lined

Fine paintbrush

1 Clip the flower stems as close to the base as possible and snip away the sepals | the green pockets on the back of the flower |. Place a flower on your prepared tray and use the paintbrush to coat with the egg white, making sure you are thorough. Brush away any excess egg white. Hold the flower by what's left of the stem over the sugar bowl and sprinkle generously with sugar. Turn it over and shake gently to release any excess sugar.

2 Do the same for the back of the flower, making sure the entire flower is coated, as this will preserve it. Place it face up on the baking tray. Repeat with the other flowers, and when you are done, put them in a cool, dry, dark place overnight or until the flowers feel crisp to the touch. Store them in an airtight container.

HONEYCOMB

Honeycomb is one of my favourite things to make in the kitchen – it's so simple to do and very exciting when it all kicks off. People talk about the science of baking but this is one recipe that will make you feel like you're actually back in chemistry class.

PREP TIME

10 minutes

COOKING TIME

10 minutes

MAKES: 200g

150g golden caster sugar
75g golden syrup
2 level tsp bicarbonate of soda

Sugar thermometer
One baking tray or cake tin at least
   4cm deep, lined

1 Place the sugar and golden syrup in a pan with a sugar thermometer attached. Set over a low heat and stir slowly | the high quantity of syrup means stirring is fine | until the temperature reaches around 150°C | the hard crack stage |. This might take 4–5 minutes, so be patient – keep a close eye on the thermometer, as it might suddenly start to rise much faster.

2 Remove from the heat, add the bicarbonate of soda and stir very quickly and evenly. It will bubble up as the bicarbonate of soda releases carbon dioxide very rapidly – this is what makes the amazing honeycomb effect. Make sure you stir well or you may be left with a bitter, soapy taste.

3 Pour the mixture into your prepared baking tray and leave to cool completely. Break the cooled slab of honeycomb into pieces to serve.

CHOCOLATE DIPPED HONEYCOMB: Melt 100g of dark chocolate | minimum 70% cocoa solids | in a double boiler | see page 196 |. Remove from the heat just before all the chocolate is melted and stir to melt completely. Break the cooled honeycomb into pieces of whatever size you like and dip them partly or completely into the chocolate. Set on a lined baking tray to cool and firm up.

SUGAR SYRUP

We use sugar syrups in the bakery primarily to flavour iced teas and coffee. Some bakeries use sugar syrups to moisten cakes, but I find it results in a cake that's much too sweet. There are some exceptions, for example the porter cake | page 66 | where the syrup flavour is very deep and bitter and adds a lovely richness to the cake, and the margarita drizzle cake, | page 65 |, where the syrup is a feature for flavour rather than missing moisture. Making sugar syrup is definitely a handy trick to have up your sleeve, especially for sweetening anything cold (that won't dissolve sugar) – such as the watermelonade on page 235. Will keep stored airtight for up to a week.

PREP TIME

10 minutes

Caster sugar

Water

Flavourings | optional – see right |

1   Place the sugar in a heavy-bottomed pan and add twice the amount of water | this should be twice the amount in volume, not weight – so if you have 1 cup of sugar, you would add 2 cups of water |. Add any flavourings now.

2   Heat over a medium heat, stirring occasionally, until the sugar has dissolved and the liquid has thickened and started to brown slightly. Remove from the heat, allow to cool a little, and remove any flavourings before using.

FLAVOURINGS: Try mint leaves, Douglas fir leaves | they make a sugar syrup that tastes like Christmas trees! |, citrus fruits, tea bags, chillies, cinnamon sticks, root ginger. You can also add liqueurs, cider, stout or spirits – just reduce the syrup over the heat for a tiny bit longer.

WATERMELONADE

The ultimate thirst quencher and the star attraction on a sunny day, especially when you add a healthy glug of vodka and plenty of ice. Decorate with a sprig of mint if you like.

PREP TIME

5 minutes

SERVES: 4

4 tbsp lemon or lime juice

400g fresh watermelon flesh, deseeded

200ml cold water

100g ice cubes

Dash of sugar syrup | optional – see page 234 |

2 large shots | 35ml each | of vodka | optional |

1   Blitz all the ingredients together in a blender with the ice cubes.

2   Stir in the sugar syrup if using and add vodka if it's a good day!

ICES

BASIC VANILLA ICE CREAM 241 • MANGO AND MINT ICE CREAM 243 • COFFEE AND PECAN ICE CREAM 243 • BROWNIE CHUNK ICE CREAM 244 • ETON MESS ICE CREAM 244 • PASSIONFRUIT ICE CREAM 244 • ABSINTHE AND MINT CHOCOLATE CHIP ICE CREAM 247 • CHILLI, GINGER AND CHAMOMILE SEMIFREDDO 248 • MULLED WINE GRANITA 251

ICE CREAM

FROZEN DESSERTS date back as far as the days of the Persian Empire around 400 BC, and early versions of chilled desserts served over ice, or sweetened ice, were made all around the globe from the days of the Chinese Emperors to the time of the Roman Empire. The ices we would recognise today came about much later – around the mid-1500s, with the advent of artificial freezing methods – and for a long time remained the privilege of the very rich. Legend has it that King Charles I had a personal ice cream maker, made to swear the method to a lifetime's secrecy so that ice cream could remain a royal privilege.

Ices are a very useful thing to have in your freezer for whipping out last minute when you are short of time. During the summer we make 'Chilly Vanilli' ice cream for the bakery, festivals and events.

DO I NEED AN ICE CREAM MAKER?

Ideally, if you're making ice cream a machine is going to make the process much easier and the results a lot smoother and creamier. If you don't have one you can make a passable ice cream breaking up the ice crystals with a fork | see below | but you might get better results sticking to granita | see page 251 | and semifreddo | see page 248 |.

THE THREE STEPS TO MAKING ICE CREAM

Making ice cream is easy enough, and involves three main stages – making up the mix, freezing and churning, and freezing to set.

1 Making up the mix. Ice cream usually consists of milk, cream, eggs, sugar and flavourings. This mix is combined as a custard, cooked enough to set the proteins in the egg and to thicken, then cooled, sometimes using an ice bath.
2 Next is the freezing and churning stage. While the ice cream is freezing, it needs to be churned frequently to break up the ice crystals and keep them as small as possible – this is what will give your ice cream its smooth texture. An ice cream maker makes this stage much easier by simultaneously freezing and churning.
3 When about half the mix is frozen it's time to transfer it to the freezer to set completely – at this stage it should be thick but still creamy. Speedy freezing will reduce the chance of large ice crystals forming.

HOW TO CHURN ICE CREAM BY HAND

1 Prepare your mix, as per the recipe, and refrigerate for 1–2 hours.
2 Transfer it into a deep plastic tub so it sits about 4cm deep and place in the freezer for 30 minutes.
3 Use a fork, spatula or hand blender to break up any frozen parts evenly.
4 Return to the freezer and repeat the process every half an hour until the ice cream is firm throughout. It may take up to 4 hours.

NOTE: Ice cream made this way is best eaten soon after making.

BASIC VANILLA ICE CREAM

A delicious ice cream with a lovely creamy texture, this is a perfect accompaniment to so many of the recipes in this book that it's worth having a batch knocking around in the freezer at all times. It also serves as a basic recipe for making a variety of different-flavoured ice creams – try adding toasted nuts or coulis, brandy or fruit. See below for some of the variations we make in the bakery.

PREP TIME
20 minutes, plus churning time
COOKING TIME
10 minutes
SERVES: 6–8

300ml whole milk
1 vanilla pod, split down the middle
8 egg yolks
100g caster sugar
250ml double cream

1   Pour the milk into a pan, add the vanilla pod and bring slowly up to scalding point – do not let it reach the boil. Cover the surface with clingfilm to prevent a skin forming, then leave to cool and infuse with the vanilla for approximately 1 hour. Once cool, carefully remove the vanilla pod from the pan and scrape out the seeds into the milk.

2   Tip a bag of ice cubes into the sink and place a large wide metal bowl on top. Alternatively place a metal bowl in the freezer.

3   In a bowl, beat together the egg yolks and sugar until thick and fluffy – approximately 4 minutes. Pour in the vanilla milk and stir until you get a thin custard.

4   Pour the mixture into a double-boiler | see page 196 |, place over a medium heat and stir continuously with a wooden spoon as you slowly bring it nearly to the boil | do not let it boil – it will most likely curdle |. When the custard has thickened enough to thinly coat the back of your wooden spoon, remove it from the heat, whisk it for a couple of minutes with a large balloon whisk | this will help it to cool quicker | then pour into your cold, dry metal bowl. Leave it to cool for approximately 10 minutes, stirring occasionally to prevent a skin forming.

5   **IF CHURNING BY HAND:** Once the mixture is cool, put it into the fridge for 1–2 hours. Remove and stir in the cream. Put into the freezer for half an hour, then churn | see page 240 | before placing in the freezer to set completely.

   IF CHURNING IN AN ICE CREAM MAKER: Once the mixture has cooled, stir in the cream, churn for 30–35 minutes, then place in the freezer to set completely.

MANGO AND MINT ICE CREAM

This is the ultimate hangover cure ice cream –
keep a batch of this in the freezer at all times if possible.

2 ripe juicy mangoes

I batch of Basic Vanilla Ice Cream
  | see page 241 |,
  omitting the vanilla pod

I tsp finely chopped mint leaves

1 Peel and core the mangoes and purée them in a food processor until very smooth. Pass the purée through a sieve to ensure you have only the thick sweet mango juice.

2 Make up a batch of basic vanilla ice cream, omitting the vanilla pod. Before churning, stir in the mango juice and chopped mint.

3 Churn and freeze as normal.

COFFEE AND PECAN ICE CREAM

One for the grown-ups; the nicer the coffee you use here, the better the flavour.
Make sure you toast the pecans.

I batch of Basic Vanilla Ice Cream
  | see page 241 |, omitting the
  vanilla pod

55ml strong espresso, cooled
  completely

75g pecans, toasted | see page 257 |
  and roughly chopped once cooled

1 Make up a batch of basic vanilla ice cream, omitting the vanilla pod. Before churning, stir in the espresso.

2 Churn as normal, then fold in the toasted chopped pecans before putting into the freezer to set completely.

BROWNIE CHUNK ICE CREAM

The brownie keeps a soft, fudgy texture and perfectly complements the smooth vanilla ice cream.

1 batch of Basic Vanilla Ice Cream
| see page 241 |

¼ batch of Brownies
| see page 147 |, roughly chopped

1   Make up a batch of basic vanilla ice cream.

2   Churn as normal, then fold in the brownie pieces before putting into the freezer to set completely.

ETON MESS ICE CREAM

Even more perfect for a summer's day than Eton Mess. This is our most popular ice cream flavour in the summertime. Serve with fresh redcurrants, berries or cherries if you have them.

1 batch of Basic Vanilla Ice Cream
| see page 241 |

50ml Mixed Berry Coulis | see page 256 |

2 medium meringues, crushed
| see page 182 |

1   Make up a batch of basic vanilla ice cream but halfway through churning, stir in the mixed berry coulis and crushed meringues.

2   Churn and freeze as normal.

PASSIONFRUIT ICE CREAM

I love passionfruit sorbet but this is even nicer – the creamy vanilla custard and sharp, tart passionfruit work beautifully.

1 batch of Basic Vanilla Ice Cream
| see page 241 |, omitting the
vanilla pod

Flesh of 4 passionfruit

1   Make up a batch of basic vanilla ice cream, omitting the vanilla pod. Before churning, stir in the passionfruit flesh.

2   Churn and freeze as normal.

ABSINTHE AND MINT CHOCOLATE CHIP ICE CREAM

This simple recipe takes a thin custard as its base and adds a good glug of absinthe, which balances perfectly with the mint chocolate chips. It's a very heady dessert, but delicately flavoured and very refreshing – great with a shot of espresso poured over it after dinner. I have served this ice cream at festivals, parties, secret supper clubs and late-night dinners in the bakery, always to a great response.

PREP TIME

30 minutes, plus cooling and chilling time

FREEZING TIME

2 hours

SERVES: 6–8

300ml whole milk

4 egg yolks

100g caster sugar

250ml double cream

60ml absinthe

100g dark mint chocolate, chopped into chips

1 Tip a bag of ice cubes into the sink and place a large wide metal bowl on top. Alternatively place a metal bowl in the freezer.

2 Pour the milk into a pan and bring slowly up to scalding point – do not let it reach the boil. In another bowl, beat the egg yolks and sugar together for 5 minutes, until thick and fluffy. Pour the hot milk into the yolk and sugar mix and stir until you get a thin custard.

3 Pour the mixture into a double-boiler | see page 196 |, place over a medium heat and stir continuously with a wooden spoon as you slowly bring it nearly to the boil | do not let it boil – it will most likely curdle |. When the custard has thickened enough to thinly coat the back of your wooden spoon, remove it from the heat, pour it into your cold, dry metal bowl and leave to cool.

4 **IF CHURNING BY HAND:** Once the mixture has cooled, refrigerate for 1–2 hours. Remove from the fridge and stir in the cream, then the absinthe. Put into the freezer for half an hour, then churn | see page 240 | before stirring in the chopped chocolate chips and placing in the freezer to set completely.

IF CHURNING IN AN ICE CREAM MAKER: Once the mixture has cooled, stir in the cream, then the absinthe. Churn for 40 minutes, then put into the freezer to set completely.

CHILLI, GINGER AND CHAMOMILE SEMIFREDDO

'Semifreddo' is Italian for 'half-cold', and in this instance is a semi-frozen custard – or a very simple homemade ice cream. Feel free to vary the flavours of your sugar syrup | see page 234 for suggestions |.

PREP TIME

30 minutes, plus freezing time

COOKING TIME

10 minutes

SERVES: 6–8

330ml double cream

6 egg yolks

80g caster sugar

200ml syrup | see below |

FOR THE SYRUP

200ml water

175g caster sugar

130g root ginger, peeled and roughly chopped

½ fresh red chilli, deseeded and roughly chopped

2 chamomile tea bags

One 23 x 12 x 8cm loaf tin, lined with clingfilm

1   Make the syrup by placing all the ingredients in a heavy-bottomed pan over a medium heat, stirring occasionally until all the sugar has dissolved. Bring to the boil for 2 minutes, then turn off the heat and leave to cool for 1–2 hours. Strain off the ginger, chilli and tea bags.

2   Whisk the cream until it forms thick ribbons. Place the egg yolks and sugar in a double boiler | see page 196 | over a low heat and whisk until the mixture is pale and thick – about 5 minutes. Remove from the heat and continue to whisk until the mixture is cool – approximately 5 minutes. Stir in 200ml of the cooled syrup one tablespoon at a time. Now fold in the whisked cream.

3   Pour the mixture into your prepared loaf tin and freeze overnight. Remove from the freezer 30 minutes before serving.

MULLED WINE GRANITA

I love mulled wine and always think it's a shame when the Christmas season is over and you're not supposed to drink it any more. Why is it that people are far more militant about eating Christmas things in season than any other type of food? We kept a variation on the mince pie (caramelised oranges, frangipane) in the bakery well into January this year, partly as a very bold and rebellious statement about freedom but mostly because we had a lot of leftover mincemeat. I like to have mulled wine in the summer with this delicious granita – you still get all the beautiful spicy flavours and it's much more refreshing. The spices used here are all optional – feel free to use whatever is to your taste.

PREP TIME

30 minutes, plus infusing, cooling and freezing times

COOKING TIME

15 minutes

SERVES: 3–4

220ml boiling water

1 Lapsang Souchong tea bag

80g caster sugar

300ml red wine | preferably a fruity, unoaked wine like Cabernet Sauvignon |

1 star anise

1 cinnamon stick

4 cloves

Juice and finely grated zest of 1 orange

Juice and finely grated zest of 1 lemon

40g raspberries, crushed | optional |

One cake tin or Pyrex dish | see note |

1 Pour the boiling water into a heatproof jug and drop in the tea bag. Leave to infuse for 5 minutes, then pour into a heavy-bottomed pan, add the sugar and heat over a medium heat, stirring until all the sugar has dissolved. Simmer for 4–5 minutes, until it thickens to a syrup. Allow to cool.

2 Heat the wine, spices, juice, zest and raspberries, if using, in another pan and simmer for 4–5 minutes. Remove from the heat and allow to cool and mull for a while – 30 minutes should do.

3 Combine the sugar syrup and mulled wine and strain through a sieve. Discard the spices and tea bag.

4 Pour the mixture into your cake tin or Pyrex dish and place in the freezer. After 40 minutes, use a fork to scrape the frozen bottom of the tin or dish. Stir the ice chips into the liquid and return to the freezer. Repeat every 20 minutes until there is no liquid left – approximately 3 hours. Break up the finished granita with a fork to serve.

NOTE: The size of the tin you use will affect the size of the granita crystals you form – a tin with a bigger surface area will freeze more rapidly and will produce larger crystals, while a smaller dish will be slower to freeze and will produce a smoother granita with smaller crystals. You can also use an ice cream tub or a bowl – anything that is suitable for putting in the freezer.

BASIC RECIPES

BUTTERCREAM

Buttercream is an icing or 'frosting' made by creaming together butter and icing sugar. Used to spread between cake layers and for icing, it can be made in a wide variety of flavours. My buttercream recipes always fluctuate slightly. The temperature of the room and your ingredients will affect consistency, which will affect how much beating you need to do and how much liquid/sugar you need to add.

TOP TIPS FOR PERFECT BUTTERCREAM

- Be prepared to deviate from the exact recipe and method. Bear in mind the consistency you want to achieve and add your sugar and liquids slowly, beating in between to get it just right.

- Use good vanilla, good butter and cream if you can – these are the flavours you want to come through, rather than lots of super-sweet sugar.

- Start with very soft (but not melted) butter and beat it alone to incorporate some air in the very first stage.

- If it's hot in the kitchen, refrigerating your buttercream slightly then beating it smooth again will mean you can thicken it up without having to add a load of extra sugar.

- If your buttercream is too thin, thicken it with butter rather than more sugar – it will taste much better. Just make sure the butter is very soft (or even melted) otherwise it will break apart into lumps and you'll have to ditch the lot and start again.

VANILLA BUTTERCREAM

MAKES: 450g

100g unsalted butter, softened
300g icing sugar, sifted
1 tsp vanilla extract
75ml double cream

1. Beat the butter alone for 4–5 minutes on high speed.

2. Add the sugar, vanilla and cream and beat on a low speed to bring it together, then turn up and beat on high for another 2–3 minutes.

NOTE: You can substitute whole milk for some or all of the cream; just add it slowly, as you may need a bit less.

CHOCOLATE BUTTERCREAM

MAKES: 550g

50g unsalted butter, softened

40g cocoa, sifted

350g icing sugar, sifted

½ tsp vanilla extract

Pinch of sea salt

30ml whole milk

110ml double cream

1　Beat the butter alone for 4–5 minutes on high speed, then add the cocoa and beat until you have a paste.

2　Add the icing sugar, vanilla, salt, milk and most of the cream and beat together slowly at first, then on high to a smooth consistency. Add more cream if desired.

CREAM CHEESE FROSTING

MAKES: 650g

125g unsalted butter, softened

200g firm full-fat cream cheese, drained of any liquid

250g icing sugar, sifted

1 tsp vanilla extract

1　Beat the butter alone for 4–5 minutes, then add the cream cheese and beat for another 2 minutes.

2　Add the icing sugar and vanilla and beat for another 2 minutes, until smooth and evenly incorporated. You can add a further 50–100g of icing sugar for a firmer frosting if desired.

ALMOND BUTTERCREAM

MAKES: 400g

55g unsalted butter, softened

250g icing sugar, sifted

4 tbsp ground almonds

75ml double cream

1 tsp vanilla extract

1　Beat the butter alone for 4–5 minutes, then add the icing sugar, ground almonds and a little cream. Beat slowly and continue to add cream gradually until you reach your desired thickness.

2　Beat for a further 3 minutes, until smooth and light.

LAVENDER ICING

MAKES: 400g

50g unsalted butter, softened

300g icing sugar, sifted

30ml lavender milk | see page 257 |

15ml honey

85ml double cream

1　Beat the butter alone for 4–5 minutes, then add the icing sugar, lavender milk, honey and double cream and blend until smooth.

COULIS

A coulis is a very simple and versatile fruit purée made with raw or cooked fruit and often sweetened. It makes a great addition to desserts like Eton Mess | see page 192 |, as its tart and fruity flavour cuts through the cream and the sweetness of the meringue. I also use coulis in Victoria sponges, | see page 45 | and Bakewell tarts | see page 102 |. You can use almost any soft fruit to make a coulis – fresh or frozen raspberries, blackberries, cherries, peaches, rhubarb, blackcurrants, redcurrants and mangoes all work well. The recipes below give rough guidelines, but feel free to experiment, combining different fruits and adjusting the sugar content to suit you.

MIXED BERRY COULIS

MAKES: 200ml

200g fresh raspberries, blackberries
  or stoned fresh cherries, hulled and
  halved, or 200g frozen mixed berries
50g caster sugar
50ml water

1   Place all the ingredients in a medium-sized heavy-bottomed pan and bring to the boil over a gentle heat, stirring continuously. Reduce to a simmer and heat for 15 minutes, or until thickened.

2   Allow to cool, then transfer the coulis to a liquidiser or use a hand blender to purée. Finally pass it through a sieve, pushing through as much of the pulp as possible and discarding any seeds.

RHUBARB COULIS

MAKES: 250ml

200g rhubarb stalks,
  cut into 1cm pieces
75g caster sugar
1 vanilla pod, split lengthways
100ml water

1   Place all the ingredients in a heavy-bottomed pan and bring to the boil over a gentle heat, stirring continuously. Reduce to a simmer and cook until the rhubarb is soft enough to crush easily – approximately 15 minutes.

2   Remove the vanilla pod, blend in a food processor or with a hand blender until smooth, then press through a sieve into a bowl.

STRAWBERRY COULIS

MAKES: 275ml

400g strawberries, hulled and halved
75g caster sugar
1 tsp lemon juice

1   Heat the strawberries in a covered heavy-bottomed pan for 4–5 minutes, or until they start to soften. Add the sugar, stir, cover again and cook for 2–3 minutes, until dissolved.

2   Blend in a food processor or with a hand blender until smooth, then strain through a sieve into a bowl and add the lemon juice.

LAVENDER MILK

MAKES: 230ml

250ml whole milk
1 ½ tsp lavender buds

1 In a small pan, heat the milk and lavender buds over a medium heat until the milk just reaches scalding point. Turn off the heat and leave to cool completely.

2 Strain out the flowers using a sieve before using.

TOASTED NUTS

Toast any nuts you like and use them to finish desserts or decorate cakes. Toasting nuts brings out their flavour and will make your dish taste delicious, even if you will be baking them into a cake - toasting (and cooling) nuts in advance will really enhance the flavour.

Nuts of your choice
Baking tray

Place the nuts on a baking tray in a preheated 180°C fan assisted / gas mark 6 oven. As there are only a few minutes in it, and toasting times will vary according to your oven, you should keep a close eye on them. Rough toasting times are as follows:

Flaked almonds: 5–6 minutes
Walnuts and hazelnuts: 6–7 minutes
Pecans: 7–8 minutes

In all cases the nuts are ready when they are aromatic and starting to brown.

FRANGIPANE

This is a versatile almond filling that can be used for tea cakes, tarts and pastries. It's a kind of simple cake mix — made of eggs, sugar, butter, ground almonds and a little bit of flour for stability — which is beaten until creamy and then baked. Frangipane is used throughout this book — I love almonds, and its very moist texture and gentle flavour works beautifully with chocolate, pastry and fruit. The recipe below will make enough frangipane to fill two 23cm tarts or 24 individual tarts. It will keep stored airtight in the fridge for up to three days and is freezable (just bring it back to room temperature before you use it).

PREP TIME

10 minutes

COOKING TIME

varies

MAKES: 850g | fills 2 × 23cm tarts or 24 individual tarts |

230g unsalted butter, room
   temperature
230g golden unrefined caster sugar
230g ground almonds
3 eggs
50g plain flour, sifted
Finely grated zest of 1 orange, lemon
   or grapefruit | optional |

1   Beat the butter and sugar together for approximately 3 minutes.

2   Beat in the ground almonds, then add the eggs one at a time, beating between additions. Finally beat in the flour and the citrus zest.

GANACHE

Ganache is a velvety mixture of chocolate and cream that is used a lot in baking to give cakes a smooth shiny glaze and to fill truffles, pies and tarts. The proportions of cream and chocolate vary depending on its use, and you can add butter, flavourings or booze to alter its consistency and taste. The quality of the chocolate will affect the texture and taste of your ganache, so use the best you can. | See page 196 for more advice on choosing chocolate. |

FOR A GANACHE GLAZE
MAKES: 400g

220g dark chocolate
| minimum 70% cocoa solids |
broken into pieces
15g unsalted butter, cubed
180ml double cream

FOR A GANACHE FILLING
MAKES: 430g

150g dark chocolate
| minimum 70% cocoa solids |
chopped into small, roughly even
pieces
25g unsalted butter, cubed
Pinch of sea salt
250ml double cream

1 Put the chocolate and butter | and the salt if using | into a bowl and set aside.

2 Heat the cream in a double boiler | see page 196 | until it starts to simmer. Your aim is to heat the cream until it's just hot enough to melt chocolate but not much hotter, so keep a close eye on it and don't allow it to boil – it's ready when it starts to bubble up just at the edge.

3 Remove from the heat and add the chocolate and butter, stirring to bring together and melt the chocolate. If necessary you can return the mixture to the double boiler very briefly, but make sure it doesn't overheat or it will split.

4 Allow it to cool slightly before spreading, piping or spooning into tart cases.

TIP: If your ganache splits, add some chilled cream and whisk hard to try to bring the emulsion back together.

BASIC EGG CUSTARD

Custard is as traditionally English a recipe as you can get. It has been around since the Middle Ages, and even today if you ask anyone for their favourite British dessert the answer will often be something 'and custard'. It is a simple technique to master but one that requires your full attention, so don't cut corners or it won't be the same. Get it right and it can form the basis of so many dishes, hot or cold, anything from ice creams to tarts and pies to trifles.

Custard is essentially a cooked mixture of milk or cream and egg yolks (the whole of an egg has the thickening properties desired in custard, but just the yolks are used for their flavour and texture) – they make the custard smooth and rich and give it its colour.

Because eggs are very sensitive to heat, a double boiler (a bowl set over a pan of simmering water, otherwise known as a bain-marie) is used to slow the heat transfer and make sure the eggs don't curdle. It can take a while for your custard to thicken, so don't lose patience or panic that it hasn't worked. Just remember to keep stirring and keep a keen eye on it.

This recipe makes a beautifully creamy custard that's perfect for pouring over desserts.

PREP TIME
5 minutes
COOKING TIME
15 minutes
MAKES: 400ml

5 egg yolks
35g caster sugar
360g double cream
Sprinkle of sea salt
½ vanilla pod

1 Stir the egg yolks and sugar together in a heatproof bowl.

2 Heat the cream in a pan with the salt and vanilla pod until hot but not boiling. You'll know it's hot when it starts to steam. Pour the hot cream over the egg yolks slowly and evenly, whisking continuously as you go. Get someone to help you here if possible – they can pour while you whisk.

3 Place the bowl over a pan of simmering water to make a double boiler | see page 196 |, and heat, whisking continuously with a large balloon whisk, until it thickens. The custard is ready when the bubbles disappear. Another good test is to drag your wooden spoon through the middle of the custard – if it is ready the spoon will leave a mark that takes a moment to disappear. It should take about 8 minutes to get to this stage.

4 Remove the vanilla pod, split it lengthways and scrape the seeds into the custard. If necessary sieve the custard through a fine mesh to eliminate any lumps, then pour into a jug and serve at once. If you're not planning to serve it right away, you can keep your custard hot by standing it in the jug in a pan of hot water and covering the top | of the custard, not the jug | with clingfilm to prevent a skin forming. If you want to use it cold, you can cover and refrigerate it for up to a day.

SIMPLE THICK CUSTARD

This is a much quicker recipe and yields a slightly thicker custard that works well for tarts. The cornflour here helps thicken the custard and shortens the time it takes, but it will leave a slight flavour that can be picked up by the savvy. The long and the short of it is, if you have the time and the inclination, use the basic method and you will have a nicer custard. But this is still a delicious alternative, and very good for when you're short on time.

PREP TIME

15 minutes

COOKING TIME

10 minutes

MAKES: 250ml | enough for 12 tarts |

30g caster sugar

2 tbsp cornflour

3 egg yolks

260ml double cream

¼ vanilla pod or ½ tsp vanilla extract

1   In a heatproof bowl, whisk together the sugar, cornflour and egg yolks by hand until light and fluffy. This works best if you whisk for 3 minutes, leave it to stand for a few minutes, then whisk again for 3 minutes.

2   Heat the cream with the vanilla in a heavy-bottomed pan until it reaches a simmer. Pour the heated cream over the egg yolks, whisking thoroughly all the while.

3   Place the bowl over a pan of simmering water to make a double boiler | see page 196 | and heat on a medium heat, stirring continuously with a spatula, until thick and creamy – approximately 7–8 minutes.

4   Pass through a fine sieve and serve immediately.

NOTE: If using cold in a tart, take the bowl off the heat at the final stage and whisk for 2 minutes to speed up the cooling process. Transfer to the fridge to set for at least 4 hours, then spoon or pipe into your tart case.

SUPPLIERS

* INGREDIENTS *

Maldon sea salt
www.maldonsalt.co.uk

Flour
www.marriagesmillers.co.uk

Spelt flour
www.dovesfarm.co.uk
www.maplefarmkelsale.co.uk

Chocolate
www.callebaut.com
www.divinechocolate.com
www.greenandblacks.com
www.guittard.com
www.originalbeans.com
www.valrhona.com/worldwide

Vanilla
www.mediteria.com

Edible flowers
www.firstleaf.co.uk (fresh)
www.greensherbs.com (fresh)
www.steenbergs.co.uk (dried)

* EQUIPMENT *

Kenwood
www.kenwoodworld.com

Pastry scrapers
www.amazon.co.uk

* DECORATING SUPPLIES *

For lustre dust, lollypop sticks, silicone jewel moulds, food colourings and flavourings, cake cases.

Squires Kitchen
www.squires-shop.com

Party Party
www.ppshop.co.uk

Surbiton Sugarcraft
www.surbitonart.co.uk

Dr Oetker
www.droetker.com

SBS Bakery Products
www.sbsbakeryproducts.co.uk

GLOSSARY

BAIN-MARIE (OR DOUBLE BOILER)
A bowl set over a pan of simmering water in which ingredients such as chocolate and eggs can be heated gently, protected from the heat of a direct flame. | See also page 196 |

BEAT
To mix ingredients thoroughly, with a whisk or electric beater, to achieve a smooth and even texture and incorporate air bubbles.

BLIND BAKE
To pre-bake the pastry for a tart, before a filling is added. The case is lined with baking paper, filled with ceramic baking beans (or dried beans) and baked for a short time to ensure that it's crisp and won't become soggy when liquid is added. | See also page 98 |

BLANCH
To cook ingredients briefly in boiling water, which are then usually plunged straight into cold water, to help separate their skins for removal.

BREADCRUMBS STAGE
In pastry or biscuits: achieved when dry ingredients have been coated fairly evenly with butter either by hand or in a food processor or mixer so that the mix resembles breadcrumbs. | See also page 97 |

BUTTERCREAM
A kind of icing, or 'frosting' made by beating butter and icing sugar together.

CANDIED
Nuts or fruits coated in sugar.

CARAMELISE
To heat until sugars turn a deep golden-brown colour, or to heat sugar until it becomes caramel.

CREAM
To beat ingredients such as softened butter and sugar together until very light and fluffy in appearance and texture.

CRYSTALLISATION
When sugar molecules reform themselves into solid crystals, forming clumps around the inside of your pan. | See also page 212 |

CRYSTALLISED
With edible flowers or fruit: coated with sugar and usually bound with egg white.

CUBE
To chop butter, vegetables or fruits into small, even cubes.

CURDLE
When a sauce separates or 'splits', usually when a mixture loses its emulsion – for instance, when too many eggs are added at once, or a mixture is heated too quickly.

EGG WASH
A mixture of egg yolk and either whole milk or double cream that is brushed over pastries and doughs before baking, to seal and give the finished bake a glossy sheen.

FOLDING
To gently combine ingredients using a spoon or spatula without stirring.

LEAVENER

A raising agent, such as baking powder or bicarbonate of soda, which incorporates gas bubbles into a batter or dough to make the finished bake risen and light.

LIP TEST

A method of checking the temperature of chocolate by dabbing a little against your lip. | See also page 197 |

KNEAD

To work a dough using your hands. | See also page 135 |

PIPE

To use an icing bag with a nozzle attached to pipe buttercreams and icings on to finished bakes or to pipe fillings into tart cases. | See also page 26 |

PROVING

To allow a dough to rise in a warm place so that it increases in volume. | See also page 137 |

SIFT

To pass flour, icing sugar or cocoa powder through a fine mesh sieve to aerate and separate clumps.

SOFT PEAKS STAGE

When egg whites are beaten until they form soft peaks that fall back into the mixture when lifted. | See also page 181 |

STIFF PEAKS STAGE

When egg whites are beaten until they form stiff peaks that hold their shape when lifted. | See also page 181 |

WHIP

To beat egg whites or cream using a balloon whisk or electric beater to introduce air and make lighter.

WHISK

To use a balloon whisk to combine and aerate ingredients.

ZEST

The outer layer of a citrus fruit, above the pith, that is grated or shaved off to act as a flavouring. Also the action of removing the zest from the fruit.

INDEX

THANK YOU...

Jenny Lord for asking me to do this book in the first place, and for all your tireless work, patience and wonderful ideas throughout the whole process

Katherine Pont for the design talent and inspiration since the very beginning

Martin Shaw for all your support and baking skills

Daisy for keeping everything together, we couldn't do it without you

Romas Foord for the beautiful photography

Rafi Romaya and everyone at Canongate

Hardwin for the helping hand when I needed it – thanks Hardy!

Peter, Christine, Lindsay and the Wrights for the help and support

Amy, Chloe, Olly and the YBFs

Luke, Rakan, Tasha, Morgan, Rose and all the Sunday bakery team

Our neighbour Augustin at Printers and Stationers for the lovely wine and the best Bloody Marys in town

Cissi, Taj and all the Swanfield girls

Sam Bompas for the inspiration and support since the very early days

Joanna McGarry for helping me get it all started

Our Columbia Road neighbours Vintage Heaven (www.vintageheaven.co.uk) and Milagros (www.milagros.co.uk) for letting us use your lovely wares as props for our shoots

David Eldridge at Two Associates

Anita King for helping me make and ice 5,000 cakes, staying up all night making cyber sugar flowers, icing gingerbreads with hundreds of screaming kids, making eyeball patterned aprons, hosting a winter witchcraft cocktail party, and all the other stupid food-related stuff I roped you into

Marawa the Amazing for the fruit salad of death, Yum Cha Cha and other collaborations and inspirations

Nuno Mendes, Gizzi Erskine, Gemma Bell, Jonathan Conway, Jon Nash, Marriages the Master Millers, Melanie Ashley, Fergus McAlpin, Jonathan Baron, Makoto and Studio Baron Design, The Calabrese Bothers, James Chase and Chase Distillery

And most of all David